C.8

D0849187

More Contemporary Prayers

More Contemporary Prayers

Prayers on Fifty-two Themes

by Anthony Coates, John Gregory, Caryl Micklem,
David Stapleton and Roger Tomes

edited by Caryl Micklem

WILLIAM B. EERDMANS PUBLISHING COMPANY
Grand Rapids, Michigan

334 01058 6

First published 1970
by SCM Press Ltd
56 Bloomsbury Street London WC1

© SCM Press Ltd 1970

This U. S. edition is published
by special arrangement with
SCM Press Ltd

Library of Congress Catalog Card Number: 79-127634

First U.S. edition, June 1970

Printed in the United States of America

Contents

Preface   vii

Attraction   1   Possessions   55
Beginning   3   Power   58
Bread   5   Preparation   60
Change   7   Protection   62
City   9   Protest   64
Community   11   Reconciliation   67
Conflict   13   Relaxation   70
Consummation   15   Resurrection   72
Courage   17   Routine   74
Creation   19   Sacrifice   76
Crisis   21   Search   79
Discipline   23   Senses   82
Education   25   Service   84
Faith   27   Shelter   86
Family   29   Simplicity   88
Fire   31   Spirit   90
Freedom   33   Testing   93
Government   35   Time   96
Healing   37   Tragedy   98
Hope   39   Triumph   101
Immortality   41   Water   103
Incarnation   43   Way   105
Inspiration   45   Witness   107
Light   47   Wonder   109
Man   49   Words   111
Mastery   52   Work   113

Index of Intercessions   115

Preface

In 1967 the SCM Press issued *Contemporary Prayers for Public Worship*, compiled by the authors of this book and two other colleagues. The reception given to it has encouraged us to attempt a further book on similar lines.

Contemporary Prayers consisted of original prayers in contemporary idiom, together with full orders for the sacraments and certain other ordinances of the church. We were chiefly concerned to explore various experimental ways of writing prayers, and although we hoped the result would provide leaders of worship with a working manual, there were gaps and inadequacies of which users have no doubt long been aware. We decided that this book should have a more deliberate structure and should provide complete sets of prayers for services. Our first thought was to put together prayers for each Sunday of the Christian year, but we were deterred by the fact that this is a period of experimentation with calendars and lectionaries. While some churches are using the Joint Liturgical Group's calendar and lectionary, others are following the syllabus of the British Lessons Council. Both follow the Christian year, and either would provide an excellent basis for a new book of prayers, but we felt reluctant to proceed while it was still not clear which cycle was likely to find the more general favour.

Our eventual decision was to take about fifty themes, and to write the prayers for services based on them. Some were suggested by the chief seasons of the Christian year, such as Preparation (Advent), Incarnation (Christmas), Discipline (Lent), Sacrifice (Good Friday), Resurrection (Easter), Triumph (Easter and Ascension), Spirit (Whitsun), though there is no reason why they should be used exclusively at those times. Other themes have been provided by the great Christian symbols, such as Bread, Water, Light, Fire; and yet others by areas of broad human concern, such as Freedom, Education, Healing, Shelter.

We have been encouraged to design the book in this way because many people are finding it helpful to approach Christian ideas through 'life themes' as well as through direct credal teaching. Such an approach is now increasingly favoured in religious education, as the Inner London Education Authority's new syllabus, *Learning for Life*, clearly shows; Michel Quoist's *Prayers of Life* owes its success to being so firmly rooted in everyday life; meditations on themes of this kind in the *Congregational Prayer Fellowship Handbook* for 1968 seemed to meet a widespread need.

The prayers under each heading are arranged in two groups, the first generally including prayers of adoration and confession, the second prayers of intercession. Thanksgiving and petition will sometimes be found in the first group, sometimes in the second. We have not, however, supplied prayers of every type each time, believing that, provided no 'part' of prayer is long neglected, it is not necessary to adhere to the full pattern at every service. We have also occasionally permitted ourselves prayers which do not belong strictly to any type. There is room, we believe, for the meditative, questioning type of prayer, as well as for the dogmatic, confident one. Prayer which always voiced an impeccable orthodoxy would be unreal. Protest against what seem to be God's ways is a very frequent motif in the Psalms.

We have not provided any eucharistic prayers. This is not because we think eucharistic worship unimportant. Nor is it because we think the canon or eucharistic prayer should be invariable. It was simply that we felt unable to write eucharistic prayers for every theme, and were unwilling to include them for some only, as if some themes were more suitable for eucharistic worship than others. We suggest, however, that when a service on a theme culminates in communion, the theme should not be left behind at this point, but be taken up and echoed in the eucharistic prayer or the post-communion prayer.

Another omission is that of responsive prayers. These would have demanded a different kind of book, designed to be put into the hands of the congregation. We also felt that responsive prayers make only a small contribution to the participation of the congregation in prayer. Worshippers will not feel that their own requests are being expressed if they merely read a part which has been written for them. Probably effective participation on the part of the congregation will only be secured if the preparation of worship is corporate.

Once again we hope that our prayers will be used with freedom. Leaders of worship should re-word, excerpt and edit them in any way they think fit. The most welcome tribute to *Contemporary Prayers* came from the person who wrote of 'the way in which it has sparked off new prayers of my own'.

Attraction

I

Father, we should find it hard to explain what has drawn us to worship today. We come to hear expressed those lofty thoughts and high yearnings which we begin to feel but by ourselves cannot formulate, and so cannot fully entertain. We are attracted by the friendliness, perhaps, or by the atmosphere of common purpose and ideal.

Whatever it is, we pray that through it you will draw us to yourself. We fail in our knowledge of you and our search for you. Worse still, we fail to put into practice what we do know and have found. We are very much afraid that it is this gap between profession and achievement that makes the church unattractive to so many.

Yet we believe that it is from within your fellowship that you chiefly work. May the cross of Christ be seen lifted up above our doubts and failures, so that men may be drawn to him even if they have been put off by us. And if you can do better than this with us, and are only waiting for us to ask, begin now again your work of transfiguring even us into the likeness of your Son. May our lives bear witness to his power and beauty.

II

Lord of creation, we thank you for the part which you have made attraction play in your scheme of things – not only in mating and parenthood, but in all those chosen friendships and preferred ways through which our lives have come to be what they now are. We are glad of a world in which people and ideas need not coerce us, and we are free to respond or not.

Yet while we give thanks we pray that we may be delivered from counting on attractiveness too much, either in ourselves or in others. May we not seek to win people to a doubtful course by conscious charm, or be misled ourselves by treating glamour as a trustworthy sign of quality.

We pray for those for whom evil has a fatal fascination, so that they are held and cannot escape, and are no longer themselves. Lord, interpose the message of your love, and break the spell.

We also pray for those who are so put off by the shortcomings of the world, their fellows or themselves, that life itself has become distasteful and every relationship is soured. Lord, let them see in Jesus what life can be. May their faith in humanity be restored by him.

We pray for those whom we dislike. Help us to love them nevertheless, and to dwell on their good points: but teach us, too, that dislike also has a place in your scheme of things, together with indignation. You do not want us satisfied with the shoddy, or smiling at injustice.

Often, Father, you confront us with that which is our duty, whether we like it or not. Let our acceptance of your rights over us kill the resentment which breeds dislike. May we welcome your will and tend ever more and more towards it.

We pray for your church, with its feet on this earth yet already feeling the pull of another world. Help your people to be faithful in their dual citizenship: and bring us all in the end to rest in the love from which nothing will separate us.

Beginning

Father, today is a day of new beginnings.

On the first day of the week you began your work of creating life out of nothing.

On the first day of the week you raised Jesus and began your work of creating new life from death.

On the first day of the week you sent your Spirit and began your work of creating new life in everyone.

Today help us to live as people who have begun again; to live today and every day with the life which comes to us through Jesus Christ our Lord.

Father, we thank you that every day you give us new opportunities to put right what is wrong, to correct some fault in our character, to do some duty we have neglected and so to demonstrate in action our trust in you.

But we let many opportunities slip by: we are so preoccupied that we do not see them, or when we do see them we are too timid or lazy to grasp them. Forgive us these failings.

Make us alert to see the fresh opportunities you are always giving us, and grant us the courage and the will to seize and use them.

II

God our Father, we thank you that the past never has the last word, that your light can pierce the darkness, and that out of deadness you bring life. We pray that the newness that only you can bring may be found in our lives and in the life of the world.

May your new life transform our work. Often we do it reluctantly or resentfully; we become bound by routine, forget the usefulness of our work to others, and lose interest in it. Help us to trust that our work has a place in your purpose, and to go about it reliably and enthusiastically.

May your new life transform our neighbourhoods. We do not bother to get to know neighbours, and then we blame them because we feel lonely and neglected. Help us to overcome the shyness and hesitation which hold us back from getting to know other people.

May your new life transform our family relationships. We can become estranged from members of the family at home; or we drift away from relatives, or offend them, and then are afraid to write a letter or call on them for fear of rebuff. Help us always to believe in the possibility of reconciliation and renewal in our family life.

May your new life transform the churches. We move forward only with difficulty because of the dead weight of the past. Give us the courage to leave behind outmoded ways of acting and thinking, and, like the first apostles, to carry with us only what we need to do Christ's work today.

May your new life transform relations between the peoples of the world. We are dogged by our history of war and international rivalry, and resentment caused by past wars and present injustice is always threatening to erupt into violence. Inspire us to establish justice, to forgive former enemies, and to break the vicious circle of war and hate.

God our Father, you are always at work creating new life. Help us really to believe this, to live constructively, and to play our part in the renewal of your creation, through Jesus Christ our Lord.

Bread

I

Lord God, we praise you.
You have always cared for the world you have made.
You have always provided for man's needs.

When the people of Israel wandered in the desert, you provided bread for them to eat and gave them water from the rock, so that they arrived beyond the river Jordan in safety.

And you have fed us, too, in our wanderings. You provide our daily food; but more than that, you have given us the body and blood of Christ, heavenly food and drink, to strengthen us to walk in the ways of love and to arrive at length beyond the river of death.

Lord God, we praise you for your care and provision for our needs through Jesus Christ our Lord.

God our Father, you have been faithful in providing food for mankind; but we have not been faithful in husbanding the world's resources or in distributing them fairly. We know that the problem of world hunger cannot be solved by our individual effort, and we have let that knowledge stop us from acting at all. We acknowledge our share of guilt. We want cheap food, and yet when we buy things like cocoa and sugar we forget that their producers go hungry because we eat cheaply. We are touched by pictures of starving children and may even be moved to give, and yet we do not urge governments as strongly as we ought to remove the causes of hunger. Forgive our apathy. Make us willing to pay more for our food if that will mean others have enough to eat. Help us to conquer that selfishness or meanness which holds us back from helping others. You have provided for the needs of all mankind; do not let us frustrate your purpose by holding on to more than our fair share. We ask it in Jesus' name.

II

God our Father, we know that you intend the whole of mankind to be adequately fed and clothed and that you have provided the resources for it. We pray now for all those who are working to put your intention into effect.

We pray for agriculturalists and water engineers and all who are engaged in the improvement of farming methods in developing countries. Give to those meeting new and unfamiliar methods willingness to learn, and give patience and understanding to their instructors when new methods are not immediately welcomed. We ask, too, that more people with technical skills may put them at the disposal of those who most need them.

We pray for politicians and civil servants and all who are engaged in the administration of tariffs and trade. Give them tenacity and determination in their negotiations and an unceasing desire to see justice established between nations. Give them firmness when criticized and the courage to promote bold and generous programmes of aid.

We pray for all engaged in the life of the church – for church leaders, theologians, and all who follow Christ. Make your church aware how pressing man's needs are. Stop her clinging to past privilege or wealth. Stop her thinking in outdated ways. Free her to serve mankind and to see that the hungry are fed. Prosper the work of Christian Aid, and may the voice of your church be clearly heard by all as a voice calling for justice.

God our Father, as we look upon your world we see deserts which could be transformed by irrigation, waste land which could be claimed for crops. Only selfishness and sin delay the time when the desert shall blossom as the rose and waters shall break out in the wilderness. Use us all in the fulfilment of that vision, for Jesus' sake.

Change

Eternal God, we believe that your purpose is unalterable love, but also that you are active, moving and making, changing things. Thankfully we affirm that your Spirit can transform people for the better, and that wherever your sovereignty is realized your creation is being renewed.

Yet we are afraid of change. We rely on known paths and settled ways. We should often like to use your changelessness as a pillow on which to rest in the middle of life's turmoil. You comfort us when we feel like that: but you show us that you can do better for us. You can keep us awake to the present and alive to the possibilities of the future. It is true, we know, that wherever we get to, you will be there ahead of us: but this does not mean that we have to resign ourselves to being carried passively along by fate. We can still make decisions which change the course of events. Within the limits set by the decisions of others, we can choose what will happen.

Father, we do not often know for sure how to apply the gospel to the choices that confront us. Keep us tending in the right direction. Give us enough confidence to choose instead of just accepting; and to back up our choice with active endeavour. But deliver us, when we do so, from that fanatical enthusiasm which makes people deaf to the arguments of others and prevents them from changing their minds. We want to be able to change when change is required, and yet not to be mere reeds bent by every wind. This we do not seem able to achieve: and we ask that your love may achieve it for us and in us.

II

Father, let your word in Jesus Christ lead us deeper into a thankfulness we do not readily feel. We cannot honestly say that we are glad that the gospel turns the world upside down. We prefer to know where we are. Yet when we consider the emancipations it has brought about, and the barriers it has broken down, we know that this has been good, even though it has cost many people their peace of mind – the peace of mind we would rather retain for ourselves today. If only we could have it both ways! But we cannot. Even faithfulness to our past decisions keeps bringing us into new and perhaps unwelcome situations: and any day we may have to decide anew. Help us to get it right.

As for all the many changes which we do not choose or instigate, but which nevertheless affect us, help us not to fear them or try to ward them off, but to accept them in Christ's name and turn the force of their onset to his advantage.

We pray for the church, giving thanks for the movements within it which are helping it to realize that part of its calling is to be an instrument of social protest and reform. Wherever Christians are still content to let religion sanctify the *status quo*, may your Spirit dislodge them, so that they may learn once again to trust you in the drift and current of affairs.

We pray for those with most power in the world to promote or resist change – leaders of the giant industrial and commercial corporations, pundits of the air and of the printed word, teachers and legislators. Help them to be aware of what they are doing, to hope and work for the best of which they are capable, and to use to the full the advances of knowledge and technology which you have given for the benefit of all.

Father, we are well aware that the day must come for each of us when we shall be changed out of all earthly recognition. May we face even this with equanimity, since we know that your Son has passed the same way without losing his identity in the change. As long as you recognize us, all will be well, and we need not worry about ourselves or those we love. Through life and death bring us to completion in Jesus Christ our Lord.

City

I

Lord God, people once thought of you as the God who had a special connexion with a single city, and a special love for it. Jesus himself longed to recall Jerusalem to you, and wept because it would not come. Christians have learned not to limit your concern to one city or one people. And yet it has been helpful for us to picture your final rule as a city, the new Jerusalem, into which all men might be gathered. We come to pray for the peace of the actual cities men live in, and for the completion of that city of yours.

We thank you for the fascination and the opportunity of city life. We thank you for its bustling activity, its trade and its culture, the scope it offers to different kinds of ability, the choice of company and occupation. We thank you that class barriers are worn away in the city, and that strangers can make their way in it. We thank you that cities are not hidebound by tradition, that new ideas can gain a hearing.

We confess the sins of the city. People can more easily be neglected and forgotten. Housing can degenerate because it is no one's responsibility. Ghettoes can spring up. Vice, violence and crime are at home in the city. What is old and valuable can be sacrificed to the new and trivial. Getting rich can be put before everything else. Habits of prayer and churchgoing can be more easily broken. Children can grow up starved of beauty and exercise and fresh air.

Father, forgive all that is wrong and lacking in our cities and help us to seize our opportunities anew.

II

Help us, Lord, to make the life of our cities more pleasing to you. We pray that we may take proper pride in them, and care for the things that belong to us all, as well as the things that are our own. We pray that those who serve on councils may follow sound policies and have the respect that is due to them. We pray that those who work in the public services may not need to envy the pay and conditions of those who work for private firms.

We pray for those who suffer in our cities: those who are ill or handicapped, those who are poorly housed, those who are unemployed, those who beg, those who have been in prison, those in any way victimized because of race or colour. May it be the pride of every city that all its citizens are treated with respect and cared for in their need.

We pray for the witness of Christians in our cities. Help us to create the kind of community in which people can feel at home, and yet to respect the need for privacy which may have brought them to the city. Help us to remember how fleeting our opportunities are, and to be always ready to listen, to help, to testify and to warn.

We pray, Lord, for your city, growing among us, yet seen only by faith. May its citizens be drawn from every nation and from every generation, including our own. May we be part of your completed city, and feel at home there, because we have sought it and loved its citizens here on earth.

Community

I

Father, we are your family, we and everyone else in the world you have made. From the beginning you have been gathering men and women into one community. You want all people to feel that they belong, and not to feel cut off because they are different from others. But we try to limit our communities to our circle of friends, to people like us, and to those of the same race as ourselves.

So you send prophets to remind us that the poor and hungry are also your children. You sent Jesus to show that your love knows no bounds of race, class, language, ideology or even religion. Always you are breaking down the barriers we erect.

Father, we are all your family; help us to realize it and live as your children should.

II

God our Father, we thank you that our individual lives become complete as we live in community with others. We thank you that together we can do so much more good than we can do separately. Yet together we also do evil things we should never dream of doing as individuals. We exclude some from our community life for selfish and unworthy reasons; we forget others because no one draws attention to their needs; we force yet others to turn their backs on the community and go it alone. Father, we pray for all those who do not feel that they belong.

We pray for the sick. We remember the physically ill and pray that the burden of loneliness may not be added to their burden of illness. We remember the mentally ill, and realize with sorrow that many now in hospital would not be there if we were a more loving and patient society. Others, who must remain there, would be made happier by visits of friends and family. Father, remind us constantly of our responsibility to the ill.

We pray for all prisoners: for those in prison for their political views, that organizations such as 'Amnesty' may give them new hope through their interest in them; and for those in prison for criminal offences, that they may not be forgotten by the rest of society, but may be helped to find a new place in the community.

We pray for the old. Save them from being cut off from others merely because they are retired. Show them what contribution they have to make to their families and others at this new stage of life, so that all may benefit from their wisdom and experience.

We pray for the young, growing up into a society which they question and against which they rebel. Give tolerance and patience to those who are older; may they listen to the protests of youth and perhaps see the younger generation exposing evils which they had not recognized or to which they had become too easily resigned.

We pray for all minorities separated from the wider community by differences of race, religion or language. Grant to all, minorities and majorities alike, understanding and willingness to accept differences and variety as part of your plan for creation.

Father of all, we thank you that all belong to your family and none is beneath your attention. Help us to love and accept others as inclusively as you do, for Jesus' sake.

Conflict

I

God our heavenly Father, we thank you for the assurance of the gospel that it is not death which has the last word, as we had feared, but your love. Yet we know that although the decisive battle has been won, the struggle has still to go on. Evil has still to be thrown out of our lives every day, for it is always moving in to re-occupy if given half a chance. Death and despair still hold to ransom those many who have not heard the news; or hearing, have not believed it; or believing it, have not yet allowed it to transform outlook and behaviour.

In our rejoicing, remind us that our fight is never simply with individuals or groups, but with the whole complex of attitudes and arrangements which make up our corporate life. Help us to admit what a hold these things have on us. But save us from thinking they cannot be changed. And where only public decision will make the difference, nerve us for the political conflict this entails.

We believe that Jesus struggled against both the darkness within and the darkness around, and that he won on both fronts. Let his victory be the motive power for all that the church says and does. So may the church be a means of renewal for all the communities and nations in which it is set. Let wrong be righted not by violence but by the knowing and doing of your will: and may all who now stumble in the dark, because of pain or bereavement or loneliness or fear, see the dawn coming up and rejoice.

II

Lord, we have come seeking the way of love, to you and to our fellow men.

We come bearing with us the agonies of our times. Our perplexity is the deeper because often enough we do not know whom we ought to be backing, and we are doubtful if our support would make much difference if we did know.

Besides, knowledge is not enough. We are burdened with the memory of all the occasions, even this past week, when we have known that something was right and have failed to do it, or have known that something was wrong and have done it all the same. How can we mend this fault in ourselves and deal with its wider effects? How are we to build your bridges in a world where better communications are making us more and more aware of the gaps? Technological advance brings men new neighbours; but it also increases the grounds for envy. Living nearer to people does not necessarily make us like them better. We had hoped that science, which already sees the world as one, would bring us towards a unity of purpose matching our unity of origin. But we seem unable to make peaceful use of our aggressive energy, or to keep conflict within the bounds of creative controversy. Lord of the two great commandments, what are we to do? How are we to love?

Some say that human nature cannot be changed, and that wars are bound to happen. Because of the gospel, we believe this is untrue: but in our own lives we have not much to show for our belief. We ask you to transform and redirect the power in our lives, so that at least in our own dealings we may give the lie to despairing assumptions. And we pray for the church everywhere, as Christians try to embody the one gospel in all the varying circumstances of different lands and cultures. Father, teach your people to seek fresh instruction from you day by day, and to learn to recognize the ways in which self-reliance meets and interacts with reliance on your Holy Spirit. Through Jesus Christ our Lord.

Consummation

I

Almighty God, our heavenly Father, when we contemplate the vastness of the universe, and the length of time it has existed, and try to conceive the purpose for which you created it, we confess ourselves out of our depth, quite unable to answer our own questions. Yet we believe you have a purpose. We believe you created us and gave us minds capable of responding to you. We believe you have given us true knowledge of yourself in Christ. We ask you to help us play the part we should in your grand design, and to complete your work in us and in all creation.

II

Lord, we pray for the universe you have made. We do not know your ultimate purpose for it, but we pray that we may not frustrate your intention through selfishness or ignorance. You have given us increasing knowledge of the universe, and more and more opportunity to use its resources as we think fit: may this make for the enrichment of its life and not for its impoverishment.

Lord, we pray for mankind. We do not know how long you intend us to continue here on earth. But grant that we may not destroy ourselves through our folly, nor waste our opportunities by perpetuating strife. You have shown us in Christ what human life might be: let it not remain an unfulfilled dream.

Lord, we pray for the course of human history. May the story of mankind here on earth more and more exhibit the influence of Jesus Christ. And may the wrongs which have not been righted here on earth be righted hereafter, except that we ask you to show mercy even on the tyrant and the oppressor.

Lord, we pray for individual men and women. We are sure that

Jesus lived and died for all men, and we cannot believe that those who died without accepting him have lost their only hope of salvation. We pray that you will continue your work with us all after we have died, for none of us yet serves you as you should be served.

Lord, we pray that we and all men may be made ready for the full vision of you. Even now, you are the best we know. What greater reward can we desire than that of knowing you more directly and more completely? Make us people who can benefit from standing in your presence.

Courage

I

Come in weakness; find strength.
Come in sickness; find health.
Come in chains; find freedom.
Come in confusion; find peace.
Come in sorrow; find joy.
Come in doubt; find faith.
Come in despair; find courage.

Come unready
Come alone;
Find Christ.

Heavenly Father,
    On our own we know that we are weak and timid: but your promises, coming to us from Christ, give strength and courage.
    He has named the devil, put him in his place, and exposed the final weakness of evil.
    He has said, 'Yes, there is truth; there is grace; there is goodness.'
    He has made us see where we stand, and what we must do, and we are surprised at the quiet strength within, which gives us the courage that does not fail.
    We give you thanks, through Jesus Christ, our Lord.

II

Heavenly Father,
    We need courage.
    Everyday crises are enough for us, and hidden fears threaten to undermine us. We find ourselves praying that certain tests should not

come our way, and hope to escape many questions. We settle for a superficial routine, and pretend that the deeper issues do not exist.

Yet, we are not content to live in this fool's paradise. We pray for the courage to be ourselves in your presence, so that by your grace we may become the people you would have us be, through Jesus Christ, our Lord.

Lord Christ,

You accepted the gift of life in faith, and lived it out with courage. You were able to walk the narrow path, withstand temptation's power, and hold fast even at the time of dereliction. Surely, you can speak as no other in this anxious age, and teach us all that courage comes in waiting patiently upon the Father. Please give us that strong courage; for are you not with us wherever we must go?

Please be with those who are lost, who simply do not know what they believe, and show them where they stand.

Please be with the anxious, who begin to despair even of life itself, and show them meaning.

Please be with those who are brought to the test, who feel tensions which rack the mind, and show them how to take one step in obedience and trust.

Please be with the sick, who are held back from the life they would live, and give them hope and perfect healing.

Please be with those who do wrong, who steal and murder and destroy, and bring them through repentance to a new way of looking at things.

Please be with the bereaved, who are face to face with the grim reality of death, and give them the generosity of spirit to entrust their lost ones to your living care.

Please be with all people who must live out their lives facing challenge as it comes, and speak strong words of courage to their troubled minds, that they may finish their course.

Through Jesus Christ, our Lord.

Creation

I

Heavenly Father,
we praise you for our birth,
    the dawning consciousness of self poised for life –
    eager for experience; yet, ready to dart at a shadow.
We praise you for our first steps in life,
    the awareness of strength in body and mind –
    exploring life's possibilities; yet, soon disenchanted and easily hurt.
We praise you for our new birth in Christ,
    the awakening to your hope beating in our heart,
    and your life flowing in our veins.
We thank you now for the eagerness which knows no fear,
    and experience which does not pall,
    through Jesus Christ our Lord.

Heavenly Father,
    You make us in your image;
        but we indulge ourselves and lose shape.
    You command the light to shine,
        but we prefer to hide in the dark.
    You have spoken and offered us life,
        but to our dismay we find that we have chosen death.
Father, be patient with us;
make us realize that our conceit will let us down,
and give us the life which lasts,
    through Jesus Christ our Lord.

II

Great God,
    You are the first word sounding in the silence of creation;

You are the light which moves over the dark waters.
You are the hidden urge bringing form out of chaos –
    the cosmic energy which organizes the very structures of life.
You are the ground of being from which man grows –
    to which he must fall and yet may rise again.
You give us pause to wonder.
    Help us become the people you intend
    and take from you our shape
through Jesus Christ our Lord.

Heavenly Father,
    You have created us to live in the light, but the eye of the world is darkened, and its spokesmen are the blind who lead the blind.

    Statesmen have to make decisions on inadequate information: their judgment is fallible. Crises are averted but there are other storms to come. Even the optimist has his fears for the future, and we get enclosed in an atmosphere of gloom.

    God, let this world see your light shine,
    through Jesus Christ our Lord.

    You have created us to live in harmony, but the tongues of the world clatter, and make our heads ache.

    Speeches and counter-speeches confuse us; talks go on; statements are issued, but nothing is settled; misunderstanding increases, and rival ideologies claim our loyalty even to the clash of war.

    God, let this world learn one language
    through Jesus Christ our Lord.

    You have created us to live in peace, but still man lifts his hand against his brother.

    We try to make amends, but our efforts to establish peace by force do not work out. As nations we need you to forgive us, and to teach us new ways of peace.

    God, let each man be his brother's keeper
    through Jesus Christ our Lord.

Crisis

I

Eternal God, for most of us today is like any other Sunday, and it follows a week which was just like many other weeks. But for some of us this is a special Sunday, because in the last few days we have realized that life is demanding a decision of us. Help us to see how typical of life this is: that for long periods at a time things continue on their course, and then suddenly or slowly they confront us with a choice.

When this happens to us may we recognize it as your doing: that life is designed to be a mixture of continuity and change; and that the Bible presents just such a story – of periodic crises, crossroads, moments for action.

So often, Lord, we substitute thinking for doing. We go on collecting our thoughts past the time when we ought to have acted – one way or the other. Teach us to be less afraid of being wrong. Help us to learn from the story of Peter that although we cannot have our time over again, even our worst decisions are not wholly irredeemable: our relationship with you can still be intact; and you will still trust us with further decisions. Make us able to thank you for the crises of life, which face us with ourselves and spur us to grow.

II

Eternal Father, we thank you for the life and teaching of Jesus. We thank you especially for the way he brought things to a head in people's lives, enabling them to discover that they could put their whole trust in you alone. Two thousand years later, the possibility of believing still comes as a crisis to us. Help us to face it, knowing that the decision whether or not to put faith in Jesus, and through him in you, is the greatest one of our lives.

We pray for those facing lesser crises: for young people as they choose their jobs and decide their way of life; for those who are embarking on marriage, or have come to some crisis in marriage; and for parents as they decide things which will affect their children.

We pray for all whose decisions affect others, whether at work or in government or in church life. May they survive the strains of power, be equal to the trust which is placed in them, and do what they think right without selfishness or fear.

We pray too for those who in the ordinary course of their work have seen that something is wrong, and must choose between drawing attention to it and letting things lie. May they be free from the fear of becoming involved; and yet free too from smugness and malice. May they find satisfaction not in denouncing what is wrong and exposing those responsible, but in stimulating what would be right and encouraging those who could do it.

Father, we are so much the people our actions make us that we ask your help, through the Holy Spirit, in the full round of our personal choices. Especially when things have gone wrong for us, when the pressures of life make us wonder just who we are trying to be, remind us that the future is always with you, who raised Jesus even from the crisis of dereliction and death.

Discipline

I

God our Father, we thank you that our lives are sometimes difficult, that we need to face hard experiences if we are to know your power strengthening us and if our characters are to be fully formed.

We thank you for the discipline of learning, for the effort required to understand a subject and to master a skill.

We thank you for the discipline of work, which can keep us alert and give us self-respect.

We thank you for the discipline of living with other people, which can counter our selfishness and call out our sympathy.

We thank you for the discipline of suffering, which can remind us how weak we are and warn us to seek what is lasting.

We accept that there is no royal road to life, that this is the only way. We thank you that Jesus, your Son though he was, submitted to these disciplines. May we who have been given so much through him not throw it away because of any slackness or carelessness, or any shrinking from the cost.

II

Father, we want to be useful Christians, always ready to do your bidding, fully equipped for your service. Help us to offer ourselves completely to you, and to form the good habits which belong to a Christian way of life.

Help us to make good use of our bodily powers. Save us from laziness, save us from overwork. Save us from dissipating our energies, save us from hesitating to spend ourselves. May our bodies truly be servants of our spirits, and may our spirits be servants of Christ our Lord.

Help us to make good use of our natural abilities. May we willingly undergo the discipline of training and practice, and put our gifts gladly at the disposal of our fellow men.

Help us to make good use of our time. Make us efficient in our work, relaxed in our leisure, attentive and approachable when other people need us. May we use to the full our opportunities for bearing witness to Christ in word and deed.

Help us to make good use of our money. Save us from the lure of money, and deliver us from nagging worries. Give us enough to meet our responsibilities and to help others in their need.

Father, we ask that we may be so disciplined in body, mind and spirit that our lives may always be useful and that in times of testing we may come through without letting you down. Help us to be faithful in little things and in big things. But do not let our self-discipline lead us into pride. Forgive our failures, but teach us through them. Remind us that the strongest can fall unless they throw themselves upon you for support. Let our strictness be a secret between ourselves and you. Give us sympathy for those who struggle and fail, and patience with those who do not even struggle.

Education

I

Lord God, you are the source, the guide and the goal of all human knowing. We praise you for the mind you have given to man, and for the whole great enterprise of discovery and reflection which each new generation inherits from the past. The light of every man is your light; and we thank you for all that nature and history teach us of reality.

Yet our responsibility frightens us. Our children's use of their inheritance depends so much on the way we pass it on. Show us, Father, how to do this confidently and not anxiously. Make us more concerned to communicate our way of looking at life than to hand down ready-made answers: and help us, as we teach, to go on learning ourselves.

We believe that through Jesus we come to know your view of human life, and your way of righting wrong. May your Spirit conform us more and more to the methods of Jesus and bring us all nearer to where he is going.

II

Father, we thank you that when we try to teach our children the meaning of life we are following your own example. You gave us the Law, to conduct us to Christ; and when we reached him, we found he was one who called and taught disciples.

Like you, he was always as good as his word. Our trouble is that our words tell one story and our actions another; and so, too often, we merely pass on our own double standards.

We pray that the church, having laid the foundations of our modern education, may play a wise and unassuming part in building upon them. We are still apt to resort to indoctrination, as if we were afraid that free inquiry might lead away from you. Deliver us from the personal insecurity which might make us over-zealous for your reputation. Show us once again that the very openness of today's outlook is of your making. Help us to trust you to keep things together even though a coherent world-view is hard for us to attain.

We pray for schools, colleges and universities; for their administrators and their student leaders. May it be the wish of those who teach to impart wisdom as well as know-how: and may those who are taught use their education to serve their fellow men and not simply their own interests. We pray that Christian families, fellowships and institutions may be conducive to a mature outlook: and we remember in concern and admiration those who are charged with teaching religion in schools where the atmosphere is hostile or indifferent.

Finally we commend to your loving care the illiterate and the educationally sub-normal all over the world. May they soon be given as many opportunities to learn as they are able to take; and may it be the aim of every educated man and woman to ensure that all may grow up without any handicap which could humanly have been avoided.

Faith

God of Abraham, we praise you, because early in history you called Abraham, and so won his confidence that he left home for your sake and struck out into the desert not knowing where he was to go. We praise you for his faith and the truth about you that he learned through his obedience.

God of Abraham and God of Jesus Christ, we praise you, because at the centre of history you revealed yourself as never before. We praise you for Jesus' confidence in you, so great that he trusted you to the end, and we thank you for the final truth about your love which dawned on mankind through him.

God of Abraham, God of Jesus Christ and our God, we praise you, because you still come to us, calling us to leave our present security for an unknown future, trusting that you will be with us wherever we go. You are with us now. Help us so to worship that we trust you more fully and are better equipped to go further along the road of faith.

God our Father, as we remember the faith others have had in you, we acknowledge that we are not people of great faith. Sometimes your promises seem so unlikely as to be laughable. Even Abraham and Sarah laughed at your promise of a son, because it seemed impossible. Yet, although their faith wavered, you kept your promise. And your promises to us are no less staggering: you promise us life of a new and lasting quality; you promise us deeper relations with others; you promise that we can be complete and healed persons. It is almost more than we can believe. Father, forgive us. Save us from concentrating on our doubts. Open our eyes to see what you can do with us, when we put ourselves at your disposal. Help us to hold firm to your promises and laugh at impossibilities as we see them becoming possible through Jesus Christ our Lord.

II

God our Father, as we look upon the world and see the evil and suffering in it, we easily doubt your goodness and your purpose. Help us beyond our doubts to faith. There is much of which we cannot be certain, and yet in Jesus we see enough to know that you love us. Help us, and all men, to accept your purpose, and, as we consider Jesus, to see by faith that nothing – no suffering, no evil – can finally frustrate your will.

By faith we see your purpose for our nation. May our national life be more and more an expression of your love. Give us a greater compassion for the homeless, the imprisoned, and all in need of the community's help.

By faith we see your purpose for all the nations of the world. May they no longer strive against one another, and may they learn to co-operate for peace and economic justice.

By faith we see your purpose for the church. May she come to live more by faith and to rely less on man-made traditions and privilege. May she be more understanding and compassionate to those who doubt, and may all who believe in Jesus and his way find a place in the community of your people.

By faith we see your purpose for each of us. Make us sensitive to the promptings of your Spirit. Help us always to accept and to do your will, however disturbing it may be.

God our Father, we walk by faith and not by sight, in the hope that the realities we do not now see will one day be visible. Help us to throw off every encumbrance, every sin to which we cling, and run with resolution the race for which we are entered, our eyes fixed on him on whom faith depends from start to finish, Jesus Christ our Lord.

Family

I

Great God,

You father us all, and embrace us in your great family of heaven and earth. We are proud to belong, and to find in it this dignity which no one can take away. But we praise you the more as we recognize Christ in our brother, wearing the face of the stranger who is hungry or thirsty, who has nothing, or who is ill, or in prison. As we do something for him we know the real warmth and affection of your family.

Heavenly Father,

It is one thing for us to know that our sinning must bring pain to someone, somewhere; but suppose it is our own parents whose life we have drained, our own brother's blood which cries to us from the ground, and our own children who must bear the shortcomings of our love? We dare not think of the trouble we have caused. Since you, as well as they, receive the smart of all this hurt, we pray that you will forgive us, repair the damage we have done, and allow us all to live again in your great family.

Through Jesus Christ, our Lord.

II

Heavenly Father,

We thank you for the pattern of family life. All experience is here from the salutation of birth to death's goodbye; and here we learn that we belong, and that we can love. But make us see that our own little family is not an end in itself, but must always be bearing the pain of rebirth into that greater family of heaven and earth from which it receives its name.

Heavenly Father,

We think of married couples, and pray that they may learn to live together in truth, and know the joy of sharing hard times as well as good. Where there is despairing talk of separation we pray for new understanding, and where the story does come to the sorry end of divorce, let it be done with goodwill.

We think of children, and pray that they may grow towards you as a flower grows towards the sun: and where their homes bear the violence of discord, may they be brave beyond their years, and become the peacemakers.

We think of brothers and sisters and relatives, and pray that they may hold together as a family, and not spend the precious years apart. Let old jealousies be forgotten, and new understanding be found; for if we do not love those whom we see, how can we talk about loving you?

Settle us happily in our families, we pray.

Through Jesus Christ, our Lord.

Fire

Eternal God, we know that apart from the sun, life on our planet would quickly cease: so we know what it means to be dependent on something. We know that the sun not only sustains our life but in one sense imparted it; that the earth is composed of the same swirling gases: so we know what it means to be derived from something.

Help us to find in these facts a parable for our faith. For even the sun's blazing power is derived from you and dependent on you. Help us to worship you, Lord, as the one who alone has the power to begin, to sustain and to end everything – the one who in making us gave us a share in your own life.

Father, we thank you for the opportunity, again and again, to confess our sins, to be rid of our shame, and to receive new hope, in the certainty of your forgiveness.

But save us from being sentimental, from thinking forgiveness is an easy thing. Help us to learn from Isaiah, who felt your forgiveness as red hot coal, how painful it can be to be forgiven. Help us to learn from Jesus, who in showing your love met rejection and death, how costly it can be to be forgiving. Make us more ready to be changed by your kindness, as metals are changed in the furnace which refines them. And help us to learn from our Lord's life that forgiveness is the very heart of love.

II

Lord God, we thank you for the beauty and fascination of fire: for the excitement it brought us as children; the crackle and smell of the bonfire; the magic of flames flickering in the grate.

We thank you for the long history of man's understanding of fire:

his discovery of it, his cherishing it, his fear and gradual harnessing of it.

We thank you for the use we can put it to today: warming our homes, cooking our food, smelting our metals and providing power for our industries.

We thank you for the fire-like qualities of human life: for the sheer energy of men; the warmth of human friendships; those who cheer us when things seem bleak; those who by their anger or indignation make us think again; men of conviction who spark off enthusiasm in us.

Yet we know that to be useful, fire must be controlled. Help us to learn from Jesus how to set fire to the earth without destroying it. Teach us to harness our aggressions and enthusiasms constructively. May we hurt only to heal, oppose only to improve, and rebuke only to encourage. And may the church, as it tries to share its belief in your love, learn how to attract without deceiving, to persuade without coercing, and to judge and convict without threatening.

Eternal God, make us more careful what we say: in case our words, like a spark which sets timber ablaze, should do what we cannot undo. May we so realize that words have this power, that we follow Jesus in his use of them, and speak the truth only in love.

Freedom

I

Lord, we have grown up to pride ourselves on our freedom – freedom to choose our own rulers, freedom to think our own thoughts, freedom to live our own lives in our own way. But we have learned from experience that freedom is a mixed blessing. In ridding us of domination by others, it puts us quite clearly in charge of ourselves. And sometimes we find that we are not fit to be in charge. We are still slaves, needing release from our fears and compulsions.

Help us to see that what we need is available to us. Not, as we first think, the freedom of mere independence, but the freedom to be sons of yours rather than slaves to ourselves. It takes us some time to consider this an advantage; but help us to see it – to realize that the freedom of your sons is the best freedom we could have: a freedom which connects us with you, instead of divorcing us from you; a freedom which limits our responsibility, instead of making it total; above all, a freedom which invites into our lives the only power we can wholly trust, the power of your love which will change us without exploiting us: so that we in our turn can treat the world in the same way.

We thank you, Lord, for the offer of sonship through Christ. Help us to realize its value, and to perfect our freedom by accepting it.

II

Eternal God, when we were children we wondered if there was anything you could not do. Slowly we realized that whatever you might do in theory, what you in fact do is governed by your love.

Help us to govern our freedom in the same way: to ask ourselves, not whether we are free to do something, but whether it would be a loving thing to do. Wean us from taking advantage of others, from thinking of life as a continual competition, from assuming that we can win only if somebody else is losing. Make us willing to restrict our freedom voluntarily for the sake of others, and to accept ungrudgingly the laws and punishments which curtail it compulsorily.

We pray for those most directly involved in deciding about liberty: for judges and magistrates, the police and immigration authorities, planning committees and appeal tribunals. May we cherish our freedoms of speech and assembly; find the right form for our laws of libel; recognize the value to society of minorities and eccentrics; and move towards a better way of dealing with offenders than simply to imprison them without treatment.

We pray that slaves and political prisoners, and all who are unjustly detained, may be freed: and that everywhere men may have equality before the law and the means to oppose governments without violence. We pray for those who in times of civil disturbance are tempted to misuse their powers, and to victimize opponents in the name of security; and for those who in times of changing beliefs are tempted to misuse their influence, either to censor opinions they disagree with, or to play upon our desire to be thought broad-minded.

Father, we thank you for the freedom you give us, with all the problems and risks it entails. Help us to use it unselfishly, and to grow in that love which both needs freedom and creates it for others.

Government

I

Your power, Lord God, made the universe and holds it in being. You are the reason for it and the ruler of it. Direct our hearts and minds to yourself, so that our humanity may be fulfilled. Forgive us for our wilful disobedience to you and for our unwitting transgressions of your commandments. Teach us that the right use of our freedom is in controlling ourselves, and in so ordering society as to encourage mutual service. Save us equally from the pride which results in lawless self-will and from the fear which results in a craven surrender of our wills to other people. Show us, in each situation and decision, how to be both our own and yours, so that we can freely and confidently enter into those binding relationships with others by which human life is shaped and supported. For Jesus Christ's sake.

II

Our Father, your church continually and everywhere offers up thanks for what you are in yourself and for what you have done for the world.

Above all, your people thank you for the gift of Jesus Christ, in whose life and death your love is perfectly made known. He did not set out to be served, or to lord it over others: his greatness was exercised in service, even to the furthest point of self-sacrifice. We thank you for his work, long ago in the flesh and ever since through the Holy Spirit, of searching out those who are off the path, urging on the lazy, giving the unruly a centre for their lives. He understands and pities human weakness. He satisfies our hunger for the truth. He strengthens us to struggle against injustice and evil.

Father, may the Spirit who comes to us because of Jesus help us to play our part in upholding, in our society, wise government and authority based on consent. Give us the sense to discover and accept the uses and limitations of organized protest. Drive us into politics, for goodness' sake: but let it be with patience and real commitment, and not just to salve our consciences by making gestures.

We pray for all in public life in our country. Show them the proper place of ambition and the desire for power, so that these things do not make them incapable of genuine service. May all who decide the destinies of men and women they never meet remember that they are dealing with human beings. And may those who control industry and commerce be concerned to increase not only financial gain but also the general benefit of more and more people.

We pray for all who live under tyrannous regimes, where government is synonymous with oppression. We do not know what to ask for them: but as they search their hearts to learn what they must do, may they at least have evidence from us and others that liberty is not always turned to a mockery by those who possess it.

We pray for men and women in the task of governing their own lives: for all with unruly tempers or desires; for those whom they harm, and for those who have to decide what is to be done with them. May realism and compassion go hand in hand, never leaving one another in the lurch: and may all who are broken and adrift find that your love can refit them for life's voyage and give them new bearings.

Father, in all these things it matters greatly who is at the helm. Help us now to put the direction of our lives into your hands. By faith we know where you are taking us, and where our Lord Jesus has gone to make ready for our arrival. Though we cannot follow him all the way now, help us to go as far as this life allows, till we are in position at the harbour-mouth, ready for the tide when the time comes.

Healing

God our Father, when we read that Jesus cured people, we cannot but be grateful; for we all want to be well. When we read that he told his disciples to do the same, and that they obeyed, we are grateful again; we thank you for all that Christians have contributed to the relief of suffering and the restoration of health.

But today we tend to leave healing to the doctors. Is it your will that the church should do this? Or should the church too be healing men by its prayers and its sacraments, as it used to before medicine made such great advances? Help us to become clear about this; and meanwhile to realize that you want men to be healthy by whatever means, that whether or not people give you the credit for healing, it is you who have given us the insight and inventiveness to heal as we now do.

Father, we thank you not only for what Jesus did, but for what healing people meant to him. We thank you that while so many people thought of disease as inevitable, as a curse of the devil or a punishment for sin, Jesus saw it as the opportunity for showing your love at work. We thank you that when he restored men to health he did so not just as a good thing in itself but as a symbol of something greater still – the breakthrough of your kingdom into human life. Help us to see it that way: to interpret the advances in medical science as symbols of something even greater – as signs of your kingdom in which everything functions healthily, within us, among us, and between us and you. And while men continue to suffer, may we help them to see how much of this ultimate healing can already be theirs, as they trust you because of the love revealed in Jesus.

II

Father, the very words we use reflect our delight at being well – hale and hearty; fit as a fiddle; full of beans. So we thank you, not only for the health we have, but for all the resources at hand to help us when we need medical attention. For the places where this is given – surgeries and clinics, hospitals and nursing homes. For those who attend to us – surgeons, doctors, dentists, nurses and midwives. For those who specialize – in our mental health, our old age, our sight and hearing. And for those who supplement the medical work as ambulance men, medical social workers, occupational and other therapists. For these, together with those whom we less often see, laboratory workers, anaesthetists and all who administer the hospitals, we give you thanks.

We thank you too for everything in our national life that protects us from illness: for inoculation and vaccination and quarantine; for the research and development of new drugs and techniques; for schemes of public hygiene, accident prevention, refuse disposal; for all the work of public health authorities, and of the National Health Service.

Father, it surprises us when we realize how many people are engaged in making and keeping men healthy. May they have wisdom as they study, patience as they work, and integrity when they grow tired or face temptation. We pray especially for those whose work is complicated by the social problems of poverty, ignorance and prejudice. Help them to decide who and what should have priority; and may what they believe sustain them in what they do.

We pray for the men, women and children who are ill; that whenever possible they may get better, and that in every case they may know they are cared for and may learn from their suffering something about themselves, about others and about you. We pray too for those who must watch their loved ones suffer. May they realize how much they can still do by relieving the loneliness of suffering, and sharing its helplessness, if need be, without embarrassment.

Father, you mean our bodies to be temples of the Holy Spirit. Help us to use them as such, seeking you, serving you, enjoying you and depending on you, through the physical life you have given us, and shared with us, in Jesus Christ our Lord.

Hope

I

Father, it would hardly surprise us to learn that you had long ago given us up as hopeless. Certainly we often feel like despairing of ourselves, when we remember the temptations we have wilfully sought out, the known danger-signals we have recklessly ignored, the harm we have done in countless ways to other people and to ourselves. This is the tale we all have to tell, and it is sickeningly familiar.

Yet you have not rejected us. Far from giving us up as hopeless, you have kept on coming to look for us. When we see Jesus eating with sinners we know there is hope for us. May his love be brought home to our hearts by your Spirit today.

II

Lord, we believe that in knowing and serving you all men can rise to the full height of their humanity.

But we do not see it happening. What we see is a world divided between the overfed and the hungry, between the comfortable and the homeless, between some entrenched in privilege and others clamorous for their rights. We see goodwill made ineffective by stupidity, and honest men failing to measure up to the demands of a crisis. We see the peacemakers and bridgebuilders pushed aside because progress towards justice seems too slow.

Yet also in this world, and identified with it, we see Jesus. We see his life of love: we see his cross. Not only as they were long ago, but as they are now, wherever his Spirit is allowed by men and women to govern human actions and purify human motives.

And so we recover faith about the world, and through faith we find hope. You, Father, are the source of this faith and hope: and you are the source of the love which alone can make the hope come true. May those who believe this learn how to avoid obstructing your love. May all who revere you make haste to promote justice and to practise compassion and to overcome the terrible strength of evil with the power of good.

Immortality

I

Almighty God,

Alone you live the life which is immortal, subject to neither birth nor death, nor any kind of change. You transcend this creation, and cannot be fitted into its ages and generations.

From this dying world we look to you in awe, knowing that it is a living word which you have spoken, and a deathless kingdom which you have brought.

Please convince us of that kingdom, and enable us to find in our life here the clue to immortality.

Heavenly Father,

Man dies, and this world dies; but nothing can bring your love to an end. Your love would grasp and hold us so that we too should outlive this world's tragedy.

Forgive us, that we have been frightened by death and parting, as if that were the final fact. Forgive us, that the nerve of our faith has broken; and that, seeing no definite answers, we have thought there was no answer, and have been overwhelmed by the futility of the things of this world.

Forgive us, and let us see that you have touched your kingdom with immortality, and called us into it.

Through Jesus Christ, our Lord.

II

Heavenly Father,

We praise you for calling mankind into sonship, to share in your timeless life.

We thank you that Jesus makes us realize this is true by his presence.

We praise you that others too, beyond death's gulf, hearten us with their love, which makes us aware of heaven, and gives us a foretaste of immortality.

We pray for man whose hope is overtaken by disappointment, and whose very striving halts in failure
   – the man who works so hard to give his family everything, and sees his eldest son end up in court;
   – the man who thinks that he will go far, and comes to realize that his best work is done;
   – the man whose life is changed suddenly by accident, curtailed by sickness, or stricken in any way.
We pray for such, who discover that this life is a dying life; that they may discover too the meaning of Easter – that their labour in the Lord cannot be lost.

Incarnation

I

With joy we worship God made man.

Lord of all worlds and galaxies, today you confront us with a wonder so great that we can hardly believe it. We knew that you were here as everywhere, an invisible presence: but it was only when Jesus was born that we found you actually sharing our human existence.

We thank you for the words of all the forerunners, in whose minds your truth had made a home, so that they could help people to be looking in the right direction for you. But for them, no one would have recognized you in Jesus.

We thank you for Mary and Joseph. But for them, your plan could not have been carried through. Beneath the stories that we have, the outline of them as people is faint and uncertain: yet we know them by their fruits, and we can praise you for the years of upbringing and training through which Jesus was brought to mature manhood.

Every home, every family, every human life has new meaning and dignity because of your coming among us. If only Christmas could have been enough to bring us back to you! We know what lies ahead for the baby of Bethlehem, and for his mother. But for that knowledge, we should not be able to see that the child in the manger is your love incarnate.

Father, the true colours of the Christmas picture have been too much overlaid for us by pious legend and pagan festivity; and on top of all lies time's thick and darkening varnish. Yet in the scholarship of critics and translators you have given us new techniques of appraisal, which can reveal the glory to us once again. Help us to make good use of these, confident that in the process we shall gain more than we lose, and that in the record of the earthly days of Jesus and his friends we may still find you and meet you face to face.

II

Father, our hearts are glad today because of the birth and childhood and manhood of Jesus. We thank you that in every phase and aspect of his life we are enabled to see yourself. He is your embodiment: the light of his character is the light of your glory.

May the inspiration for our worship and obedience come from him. May the church fulfil its calling to be his embodiment. In each Christian may Christ be incarnate by faith, so that his light may shine before men through us all, and his glory become the ground of praise to you from the whole world for ever.

We pray at this Christmas time for our world made callous by the endless parade of other people's anguish. A world where at fabulous cost man reaches for the moon, but boggles at sixpence on his income tax to feed the hungry or house the dispossessed. A world in which the arts of publicity can make any point of view seem plausible, and in which it is usually the personal quest for power that sets the pace of a man's service of his fellows.

Father, the birth of Christ convinces us that you are in the midst of all this, carrying on your strange and holy work of new creation. Help all who care about it to avoid hindering it. We know that our activities are for ever making incarnate our own mixed motives, and we see our defects reproduced in our children. We pray that your Word made flesh may prove a more powerful influence than our bungling example or genetic legacy; and that through the symbols and sacraments which give body to your living truth, many today may recognize and embrace it.

In the name of Jesus Christ our Lord.

Inspiration

I

Eternal God, we thank you for the way you have disclosed yourself to us: supremely through Jesus, in the human life he lived, in his death and resurrection; yet also in Israel, where there was preparation for his coming; and in the church which has drawn its life from him ever since. We thank you too for the other religions practised in the world, for those outside the church who discover and declare what is true. We thank you that in every part of mankind's story you are at work and can be discerned: that even in the make-up of the universe, in the majesty and terror of its size, in the beauty and the harmony, the flux and variation of its processes, traces of your purpose can be found and recognized.

Give us a greater confidence that you are active in every event, and in all aspects of every event, and that nothing evades your knowledge and care. Help us to be certain that in every situation we can turn to you: that because you are linked with our hardship and heartbreak, pain can help us rather than harden us; that because you are linked with our joy and achievement, we can avoid a false pride and a false security. Bring us to see that no situation in life, no discovery about the universe, no insight into the nature of man or the course of history, need turn us away from you or make us despair of you. For this is your world, and although you transcend it you rule it from within.

II

Lord, we thank you for the amazing variety of shape and texture' colour and sound, which the world contains; for the charm which the bodies of living things display; and for the genius of artists who see all this and reflect it in their work. We thank you for painters and sculptors, poets and dramatists, and for all who by their composing and performing distil and interpret life's beauty and truth. Save us from neglecting and abusing what is beautiful; yet save us too from pursuing it in isolation from everything else that makes for human enrichment.

We thank you for the evidence that artists give, that so much of their work depends on inspiration; that their discipline and skill are merely servants of what prompts them from within and grasps them from outside. May we respect what they say, and sympathize with their difficulty in saying it, as we try to understand your way of governing the world.

For we know from the life of Jesus that you bring about your kingdom not by crushing or compelling but by showing and convincing. You elicit our trust and obedience not by towering over us but by living beside us. You operate as spirit not to bludgeon us but to stimulate us, persistently yet patiently, fostering and promoting your will without defeating or belittling us.

Lord, may the church be content to make itself felt in the world in the same way. However confident we may be that through the Bible and the Christian faith we have true knowledge of you, save that confidence from being arrogance. Remind us that our insight and experience are due far more to your grace than to our efforts. And help us to admit that although many men fail to worship you, they may none the less be inspired by you in their courage, their compassion, their integrity of mind and their striving for what is right; and that even where your presence is unnoticed or your very existence denied, there too you can instigate good.

Forgive us, Lord, for thinking that as Christians we have superior standing in your sight. For we know that in Jesus you have identified yourself with all humanity, and that in the spirit every human life is under your intimate care.

Light

I

Heavenly Father,
    You come as the light in the morning bringing in the new day –
        the light in humanity bringing forth the new man.
Please disperse this world's night, and make us children of your day.
Through Jesus Christ, our Lord.

Heavenly Father,
    Man goes on sinning.
        His very sight is darkened and in his grey world he stumbles
           because there is no way.
        But your light burns in Christ to fill mankind with a burst of glory,
           and your world comes to view, a vision of splendour:
    man goes on living.
We thank you for your light which floods our soul, and pray that we
    may find our way with Christ.

Heavenly Father,
    We are afraid of your light.
        It is too searching, too bright, and we do not want its beam upon
           our private life and secret thought.
        We confess that we look for hiding places, and run even into the
           night.
    Nonetheless, search us out.
        Shine your light upon us.
        Expose our guilt and make us face it.
        Bring us to the reckoning of your love.
        Forgive us, and help us to bear your light.
Through Jesus Christ, our Lord.

II

Heavenly Father,
    We know what it is for darkness to close in on the mind,
        for the horizon of thought to narrow,
        for the circle of concern to contract,
        even for the light within us to fail as if the batteries were flat.
We think of all whose existence is bound within the darkening confines
  of their own world.

    But we know also the source of light,
        your Word in Christ that makes it shine –
          to charge our thought,
          and speed it into the expanding realms of your creation
          where the morning stars sing together, and the sons of God
          shout for joy.
We pray that all men and women, young people and children, may
  know the glory of living within your boundless kingdom.
Through Jesus Christ, our Lord.

Man

I

Heavenly Father,
    We praise you for mankind –
        born to give, and born to receive;
        born to help, and born to be helped;
        born to lead, and born to be led;
        born to forgive, and born to confess;
        born to love, and born to be loved.
    We think that we can live on our own and ignore the Lazarus at our
        gate; but we put ourselves on the wrong side of the great gulf, and
        find that we have chosen but an affluent death.
    Make us understand that we are part of each other, born together
        within your family to know the warmth of human ties.

Heavenly Father,
    We praise you for Jesus –
        born of you in the kaleidoscope of history to be the true pattern of
            man for all time.
        He is man – son of man – real man.
        The light which shines in him is our light, and the life which
            throbs in him is our proper life too.
    We praise you for man –
        designed for more than we thought
        and stamped with the pattern of Christ.
    We thank you for this great potential which we have
    through Jesus Christ, our Lord.

II

Dear Lord, who is my neighbour?

He is the man next door.
When he is ill
he coughs in the night, and I hear him spit.
He lets himself go, and is a nuisance because he does not eat, and grows thin – and what will become of him?
When he is well
he is the first to get up, first to mow the lawn, first to paint his house, and first to clean his car.
Day and night I hear his life: he is so close to me.
He is too close to me.
He is near to me: in fact, he reminds me of myself.
He is flesh of my flesh and bone of my bone.
I wish he would go away, because he troubles me with his joys and with his sorrows.
But he must not go away. He is the reflection of God to me, and without him I cannot live.
Father, teach me to know my neighbour, and to love him,
through Jesus Christ, our Lord.

Heavenly Father,
We reckoned that we were men living in a man's world – that we knew human nature, and needed no one to tell us about life. But Jesus gives us a clearer view of life's possibilities, and shows us what it is to be truly human.
We admit that by our ignorance, prejudice and exploitation we have reduced man's stature, and robbed life of its splendour.
Father give us back our glory, through Jesus Christ, our Lord.

Heavenly Father,
You set before mankind the possibility of life and good; but we are afraid that he is choosing death and evil.
In fear, nations build up armaments to defend themselves against attack; hostile missiles are already aimed at the great cities, and the whole world could go up in one lunatic moment.
In selfishness, nations eat and drink more than is good for them,

and indulge in every kind of luxury, while millions die of hunger
and want.

In ignorance, nations foster prejudice against minority groups, and
inflame racist feeling, which expresses itself in persecution and
murder.

We pray, at this eleventh hour, that mankind may rise as one to
repudiate these murderous and suicidal follies, to do good, and to
choose life by taking the road which was opened at the cross, through
Jesus Christ, our Lord.

Mastery

I

Lord God,

In your creation you span the distances of space and time;
You hold the universe in the hollow of your hand.

Where does your power originate?

You have brought forth man in the evolution of your purpose;
You have achieved man to perfection in Christ –

He is the very expression of your mind,

and bears in himself the stamp of your authority.

Where will your mastery end?

We pray that we may accept your control over our lives and find fulfilment in your plan.

Through Jesus Christ, our Lord.

Heavenly Father,

We are thankful for the honour to which man is called. You put power in his hands and give him a world to subdue, so that he has a share in your work of creation.

We thank you for all the discoveries of modern science

– of medicine and surgery, giving him some power over life and death;

– of nuclear physics, enabling him to harness the power of natural forces, to reshape his environment and change his mode of life;

– of space research, giving him vision of other worlds to win.

We give you thanks for man's ambitious spirit, and pray that as he tames the forces of the universe, he may hear the morning stars of creation singing your glory.

Through Jesus Christ, our Lord.

II

(We suggest that sometimes the division is made at (II) below, instead of at this point.)

Heavenly Father.
>We confess that man accepts the powers which you give and misuses
>them for his own selfish ends, to the spoiling of life and the
>corruption of his soul.
>He discovers creative power in the atom,
>>and makes a bomb.
>He learns how to control bacteria,
>>and experiments in germ warfare.
>He invents the motor car and aeroplane, computers, transistors and
>television sets, concrete and plastic,
>>and turns them into tyrants his way of life must serve.
>In pride he overreaches himself,
>>and in complacency disengages from the rhythm of your creation,
>>and entombs himself in a world of his own making.

Father, we pray that you will school us to your will, and teach us the
mastery which is responsible and creative.
Through Jesus Christ, our Lord.

(II)

Heavenly Father,
>You give man responsibility which he must exercise, and call upon
him to make decisions at the risk of making mistakes. We remember
all who are brought to such a test, and find themselves on their own.
>We remember scientists of all kinds, who know that the results of
their work could become a blessing or a curse. We pray that they may
be careful not to be compromised in evil experiments; that they may
put their trust in revealing the truth; and that they may keep their
integrity in whatever dilemma they may find themselves.
>We remember those national leaders who alone have access to con-
fidential information, and must make up their minds what course of

action to take. We pray that they may have a just motive, clear judgment, and consistent thought.

We remember educators, preachers, leaders and speakers of all kinds, who have power to influence opinion. We pray that they may always remain servants of the truth, and not try to manipulate people's loyalty.

We remember industrialists and employers, whose decisions affect the lives of millions. We pray that they may insist upon quality in production, and provide good conditions of work; that they may be honest in their dealings, and never become cynical about power or treat it as a game.

So we pray for many who bear the burden of responsibility, that they may accept your guidance and be very wise.

Through Jesus Christ, our Lord.

Possessions

I

Father, we give thanks to you, the maker and owner of the universe for the fact that we too can possess things. Whether we have worked for them or been given them, whether we own them ourselves or share them with others, we thank you for all our possessions: for the enjoyment they give us, the security they provide, and the way they enable us to express our personality

Yet we have to admit that they often play havoc with our character. They can make us envious, when others have more than we have; or resentful, when others want as much. They can make us anxious, when our wealth seems to be threatened; or smug, when things have gone well for us. They can make us behave in ways we deplore: they can make us tell lies, take unfair advantage, even pretend that others do not exist. Above all they can make us possessive towards life in general, and deceive us into thinking that getting richer is the main aim of being alive.

Father, the world you have made is so capable of becoming rich that we cannot believe that you mean us to be poor. But help us, as we enjoy the world's increasing wealth, to treat our possessions as a dangerous privilege and a weighty responsibility, and to realize how easy it is for men to be not only wicked but stupid, content to be wealthy and no more. May we possess our possessions and not become possessed by them, since we know that whatever belongs to us we are only well-off because we belong to you.

II

Father, it sometimes seems hard to believe that you mean us to be equal. We are born with different abilities; we face different opportunities; and we live in a world where one of the main incentives to effort is the promise of unequal rewards.

Yet we cannot believe that you mean us to trade on our inequalities or to increase them. For in Jesus you have challenged our normal values. You have told us that the last shall be first and the first last; and that he who is great must be the servant of all.

So we thank you for everything in our national life which is aimed at removing our inequalities and compensating for them: for the health service, which shares the cost of illness among us all; for state education, designed to ensure that each child gets the schooling he needs; for social security, which helps us in old age and in times of need; and for the schemes of taxation which finance all this, and redistribute our wealth more evenly. As we thank you for all these things, we pray for those who devise and administer our welfare and taxation. May they be both humane and efficient; and may we neither resent being taxed nor resent being helped, but come to share the ideal that our welfare State embodies.

We thank you too for the efforts now being made to even out wealth on a world scale: by increased government aid to developing nations; by reduction of waste and corruption in those countries themselves; and by changes in the trading and currency arrangements which hit hardest those countries with least revenue. We pray that the richer nations, including our own, may be willing to forgo some of the advantage a competitive world gives them; and that the individuals in government and commerce who have to make particular decisions about this may be willing to risk some unpopularity for the sake of international justice.

Father, we pray for ourselves, that the positive role of the State in our lives may not kill voluntary service. May the churches be active in recognizing new needs, pioneering new services, and helping in those cases where state aid is either impracticable or unacceptable. And may church members, in their work and their church life, disarm people's fear that equality dries up initiative. May we find our incentive, not in the thought of outstripping others, but in the thought of pleasing you. As we remember what you have already done for us, may the wealth we most desire be the wealth we already have, for which we need not compete – the wealth you have given us in Jesus Christ, who was rich and for our sakes became poor, so that through his poverty we might become rich.

Power

Eternal God,
  You are the power behind all things . . .
  Behind the energy of the atom,
  Behind the heat of a million suns.

Eternal God,
  You are the power behind all minds . . .
  Behind the ability to think and reason,
  Behind all understanding of the truth.

Eternal God,
  You are the power behind the cross of Christ . . .
  Behind the weakness, the torture and the death,
  Behind unconquerable love.

Eternal Power,
  We worship and adore you.

Father, source of all power, we confess that we do not always use the powers you have given us as you intend. Sometimes we are afraid of the power we wield, and so do not use it at all; at other times we are careless in our use of it and harm others; at yet other times we deliberately misuse it to achieve our own selfish ends. We confess our misuse of our God-given powers, and ask for your grace to use them properly in future.

II

God our Father, we thank you for the powers that man has at his disposal, and yet we know that these powers are a mixed blessing, because of their possibilities for evil. Do not let us be afraid of them for that reason: help us to reassert our mastery over them.

We think of the power of the nations of the world. In international affairs it so often seems that events are out of our control, and rule us. Father, help us to see how national power can be wielded for the fulfilment of your will.

We think of the power of economic systems. Often we feel enmeshed in a system which is not fair and yet cannot be changed without causing immense hardship. Father, help us to become masters of economic forces and to order them for the purposes of justice.

We think of the power of governments. They now touch our personal lives at so many points. Father, may politicians and civil servants use their powers responsibly and respect the rights of individuals. Give us the courage to challenge them when they are wrong, and willingness to share in the processes of government ourselves. May the power of governments everywhere be used for the good of all.

Father, yours is the ultimate power. We see evidence of it everywhere in the world of things and men, but most of all in Jesus Christ. In him we see the power of your love: weakness and death did not destroy him and you raised him from death. May that same power of love be in us.

Preparation

I

God our Father, as Christmas time approaches we have a lot to get ready. There are presents to be bought and wrapped, greetings to be sent.

Never let us forget to prepare our own hearts for the time of your coming. What will be the good of all our activity if it crowds you out, or of our gifts and greetings unless our own lives are presentable to you and to other people?

Not that our trying to put a fair covering on ourselves would be any use. You know us too well for that. We can only ask that you will make the best of us. At least with your help we can see to it that other people receive the presents you have told us to deliver to them – gifts of love, and joy, and peace, and hope – food for the hungry, houses for the homeless, welcome for the despised.

God our Father, there is more to get ready than we realized, and time may be shorter than we think before we are called to account. May our praise now give new zest to our stewardship: for Jesus Christ's sake.

II

Father, we praise you, great above all earthly greatness, loving beyond all earthly love. From you comes everything that is good: your mind thought of it, your word brought it into existence. We thank you for our life, and for the centuries upon centuries of human history and achievement that we inherit. Especially we thank you for the Jewish people, and for the true religion which you called into being among them to lead, as we believe, towards Jesus.

Yet something has gone wrong, Lord. We started out so well. In man's infancy, his vigorous self-assertion is matched by his dependence on others. Why can we not recover that balance in our maturity? As it is, the factiousness which keeps erupting among men threatens to destroy all the good which their frail co-operation is trying to build. In despair we begin to prepare for the worst instead of for the best.

Father, when in our short-sightedness we miss our footing, and our selfish bias begins to topple us towards the chasm below, save us and set us right. Prepare us to make the next new stage of the journey, not one by one but together. And then, if there are places where the route is hard to find, help your task-force of Christians to make it clearer for people to follow. Let us be well known for opening up possibilities in the name of Jesus.

Renew our respect for all whom in any way you have put on the alert for signs of your presence and your will. Recall us, with your whole church, to the task of making the world fit for you to live in – you and your family.

Protection

I

Lord, we are often afraid.

We know what the Psalmist means when he says, 'As for me, I almost lost my foothold. I nearly fell.'

Yet we envy him too. We would give a lot to be able to believe that you stand up for us, and therefore we are safe; and that when we come to our agony you will give your angels charge over us, to bear us up on their hands.

What do you mean by telling us not to be afraid?

We can believe that we need not be afraid of *you*: and we have Jesus to thank for that faith. But how are we to attain to the perfection of love which casts out other fears too?

And although no doubt it is true from your end that nothing in life or death can separate us from your love, it mostly does not feel true from our end. Even the very edge of the shadow of death is enough to make us feel cut off from light and air.

Save us, Lord, we beg you. May the rescue which you have made true in Christ be true in our own experience too. For his love's sake.

II

Lord, we wonder whether we are supposed to look to you for protection or not.

Do you really keep a fatherly hand on us, or have we been imagining it?

If you really do, we cannot help feeling puzzled as well as reassured. What about the others, who have suffered disasters which we have escaped? We are sure it is not because they are unbelievers, or greater sinners than we are. Is there perhaps a safety-net further down the abyss than we can see? Will everyone be caught there and drawn to firm ground by everlasting arms?

If so, Father, we ask you to help all who believe this to convince their fellows that there is hope, especially those now falling into despair because of war, disease, famine or old age.

Jesus fulfilled the promise you had made through the prophets that you would search out and save your lost and bewildered sheep. As we read the gospels we see him doing it, and we hear him saying that each rescue makes you glad. If you really know every one by name, and nothing can snatch them out of your hand, then we are safe whatever happens. Lord, we believe: help us where faith falls short. Help us to recognize your voice wherever we hear it, and to follow, confident that time and eternity comprise a single fold, with one shepherd, and that you will bring us home.

Protest

I

We thank you, Lord God, for the dignity you have conferred on human beings, by making them in your image and giving them the help of your Son in their need. We thank you for the rights we prize for ourselves and accord to others:

the right to survive once we are born;
the right to be educated;
the right to work for our living as free men;
the right to marry and bring up a family;
the right to speak and think for ourselves;
the right to be protected by the law;
the right to take part in the government of our country;
the right to rest and the right to travel.

We thank you for all who in the past have struggled to win these rights for themselves and others: for the prophets who have sought to arouse the conscience of nations, and for the pioneers who sacrificed life, liberty or prospects in the cause of social reform.

We confess, Lord, that not all men possess these rights as fully as they should. The right to live is taken away; freedom of speech and freedom of thought are suppressed; many do not receive a fair return for their work; many are denied their rights because of their race or colour or sex or conviction. Lord, forgive us for all the ways in which, directly or indirectly, we deprive others of their rights. Forgive us for honouring dead prophets and persecuting living ones. Forgive us for paying lip-service to the ideal of human dignity and undermining it in practice. Teach us to be alert and sensitive to the voice of protest in our own time, and to speak and work in the cause of the under-privileged, even though it means sacrifice.

We who are surrounded by voices raised in protest bring before you, Lord God, the wrongs which our fellow men suffer.

We pray for those on whom are inflicted the cruelties of war: those who are killed, maimed and made homeless by bombing and fighting; those who are raped, robbed and tortured by members of occupying forces; those who are brutalized by what they are ordered to do; those who are forced to fight against their conscience. Forgive us that we have ever thought that war justifies these things, and give us new determination to prevent such miseries.

We pray for those who are denied their liberty: those imprisoned or detained for no crime but their political or religious views; those compelled to live and work as slaves; those denied access to education and sources of information. Make us less afraid of ideas which challenge our own, and help us not to require of any man service on terms that we should hate to have imposed on us.

We pray for those who are exploited, and do not receive sufficient payment for their work. We pray especially for the poor of Asia and Africa, Southern Europe and Latin America, from whom we buy food and raw materials more cheaply than we should. Show us how we can influence those who determine the terms of trade.

We pray for those who have little chance of sharing in the government of their country: those who have no vote; those who have no choice of candidate; minorities which are not strong enough to elect representatives. May leaders everywhere become accountable to those they govern, and may democracy neither be stifled by inflexible systems, nor be manipulated by powerful factions.

We pray for those who are at the mercy of economic systems: those who are unemployed or live in fear of redundancy; those who must make things that will quickly wear out; those who must persuade others to buy what they do not want; all of us as yesterday's luxuries become today's necessities. Lord, help us to live simply and generously and to do work of which we need not be ashamed.

We pray for those who foment and organize protest: those who lead marches and sit-ins and unofficial strikes; those who rouse opinion by their speech and writing; those who wait in prison for their moment. Make them willing first of all to persuade, to appeal to the judgment and the conscience; help them in the decision whether to use violence to right an extreme wrong; preserve them from corrupting those whose cause they take up, from destroying some while they liberate others.

We pray for those who have to deal with organized protest: the government, management and union leaders, university administrators, the police. Help them to take wise decisions and to implement them diplomatically. Show them when to yield to pressure and when to stand firm. Save them from using brutal methods in the heat of the moment. We pray that no issue may be decided by violence and terror but that the just cause may be strong and in the end prevail.

Reconciliation

Lord and Father, we worship you as the God who has made us. Life is your gift, and in you we live and move and exist. You know all our needs, and you meet them generously. Nothing can separate us from your love.

And yet we have to confess that we pass our lives in fretful discontent. We are never satisfied with what we have, but must always envy others their money or their success. We cannot allow other people to be different from us: either we want to be like them or we try to make them conform to ourselves. We are not content with the approval of conscience: we want the esteem of others as well. We twist the truth until it fits in with our ideas. We shrink from suffering, and grow impatient under it. We are full of worry about the future, afraid of monotony, afraid of change.

We know that we are greatly to blame. We know that we could have been less discontented. But we cannot change ourselves enough to be really reconciled to life. We cannot be different unless you take us in hand and help us to grow into new people.

We know that you once gave men through Jesus the assurance that they were reconciled to you, and in this way they became reconciled to life. You have renewed that assurance to generation after generation since. Reconcile us as well. Come to us in mercy, and awaken our faith

II

Christ died that we might be reconciled to you, Father, and to one another. People cannot believe in reconciliation with you unless there are human reconciliations which reflect it. And so we pray for the healing of the broken bonds of human life.

We pray for reconciliation between nations. We do not believe that the true interests of nations ever conflict sharply enough for war to be necessary. And yet we know that peace has often been exploited by those who love to oppress, making war a grim necessity. Give us true peace, founded on justice and respect for human rights.

We pray for reconciliation between races, especially in countries where different races live side by side. May the principle of equal citizenship and equal opportunity be accepted everywhere. May the laws strengthen the hands of people of goodwill. May different races learn to speak the truth in love to each other. May wisdom and patience mean that the day of bloody revolution need never come.

We pray for reconciliation between generations. It is hard for parents to realize that their authority is not absolute and that their values may be questioned. It is hard for young people to realize that they lack experience and may have no more staying power than their elders. It is especially hard when one generation is given opportunities and choices the other did not have. Grant, Lord, that both may learn from each other, and that the common problems of our world may be faced together.

We pray for reconciliation between the sexes. We thank you for the new opportunities women have to follow their careers and take part in public life. Help men and women to understand the ways in which their roles have changed and must change, and to work together on equal terms and with mutual respect. Help husbands and wives to achieve harmony in marriage, despite the stresses of modern life.

We pray for reconciliation between churches. Break down the inertia which keeps us apart when the original causes of division no longer matter. Help us to judge whether present differences are sufficient to be allowed to obscure the unity we have in Christ. And may unions of churches take place in such a way that they do not become the occasion for new divisions.

We pray for reconciliation between religions. May those who profess one faith no longer suspect and misrepresent those who profess another. May good be recognized wherever it exists. May all men hold to truth as they see it, and bear witness to it, but with goodwill and respect.

May the Christ who once reconciled Jew and Gentile, slave and freeman into one body continue to break down the walls which divide us.

Relaxation

I

Lord, you have created us so that we need regular periods of rest. The work of the day must be followed by the sleep of the night. A day off each week is precious and necessary to us. After long stretches of work we need holidays. We believe that these conditions of our life are an expression of your will. For Jesus recognized our need for rest; and one way people have thought of life after death is as the everlasting rest of your people.

And yet we know that relaxation is not just a matter of stopping work. Some of us quickly become bored when we are not working. Or work has left us so exhausted that we cannot enjoy our leisure. Or other people make heavy demands upon our spare time. It seems selfish to insist on time to ourselves, but we cannot be ourselves without it. We do not want to consume our time and energy on trifles, and yet if we cannot sometimes forget all about ideals and need and service we find we have not been refreshed after all.

Father, guide us in this as in other things. Help us to relax as we should, knowing that the world is in your hands, not in ours. And take up our leisure time into your purpose, so that when we begin our work again we do so the better for having rested.

II

We thank you, Father, for all there is to enjoy:
    the beauty of land and sea and sky;
    the companionship of pets and the fascination of wild life;
    the society of other people;
    conversation, dancing, games and exercise;
    the wit and wisdom of men;
    crafts and hobbies, literature, music, painting, plays and films;

the pleasures of recollection and the excitement of looking forward;
the services of the church, the life of the spirit here and now, and the
hope of the full life to come.
For all these things we thank you, Lord, and ask that all people shall
have their chance to enjoy them.

We pray, Lord,
for those who carry great responsibilities, that they may be able at
times to shed their load and enjoy leisure;
for those who have to work so long or so hard that they have little
leisure, that they may successfully struggle for better conditions;
for those who have time on their hands, that they may have the
chance to occupy themselves and be useful to their fellows;
for those who provide entertainment for others, that they may set
themselves high standards, whether success comes easily or not;
for ourselves and other Christians, that we may use Sunday wisely
and find the best way of safeguarding its value for all men.
Help us and all men, Lord, to find that rest and peace which you can
give us, whatever our circumstances – the peace which comes from
following Jesus Christ as Lord.

Resurrection

I

Heavenly Father,

We tremble on the threshold of this day's wonder, lost for words. Like the disciples we dreaded that Jesus' life had come to nothing, and we did not expect to find him: but he startles us with a greeting and disturbs us with his presence. It is not that we should have forgotten him. We were determined to hold him in our memory and cherish his example, but now he is no mere remembered friend; he is someone who meets us and guides us still. Father, we praise you for his resurrection – unexpected new creation.

You have raised him from the dust of death, and breathe sweet life into the graveyard of this world. Suddenly life has just begun, and we are moved at its great prospect.

Fill us now with the joy of believing.

Through Jesus Christ our Lord.

Heavenly Father,

Jesus has broken out of the tomb and gone ahead of us into the world: but we try to lock him in our churches, to display him to outsiders as we think fit; or take him on our pious excursions as if he belonged to us. How pathetic! How futile!

Please forgive our condescension, and end our conceit.

Through Jesus Christ our Lord.

II

Heavenly Father,

We hear the news that Jesus is raised from the corruption of death, and walks this creation as the Prince of Glory. We pray for this tired old world with its drugged illusions, that it may awaken to the new morning, and shine in your splendid light.

We pray for men and women who have compromised with evil, and find themselves on a downward path into the frightening dark.

We pray for those who have lost their sense of wonder, and expect no new idea; who no longer argue with their friends, and find that no answer is given to those who have given up asking questions.

We pray for those who have achieved the security they sought, but find themselves disappointed with only a semblance of life.

We pray for men and women who receive life with all its promise, and succeed only in burying it in the ground.

Please make us understand that as you raised Jesus from the dead you can recreate us to live in true glory.

Through Jesus Christ our Lord.

Routine

We will praise you every day, our Father, because every day you renew your kindness to us. Day by day you give us our daily bread. Day by day our inner nature is renewed, despite the wear and tear of daily life. Help us to take up our cross daily and follow you.

We thank you for the way the world makes our life possible. We thank you for the life which sustains our life, and for the materials we can use. We thank you that day and night and the seasons return so predictably, allowing us to plan ahead. But we thank you too for the variations which surprise us with novelty, the changes that remind us that we are not here for ever, the deprivations which give us back the healthy pangs of desire.

We thank you for making us dependent on other people for birth, for upbringing, for company, for stimulus, for help. We thank you for their labour, particularly for those who serve us every day. And we thank you that in our turn we can serve them and find daily satisfaction in helping to meet their needs.

We confess, Father, that we are slaves to our established habits, unwilling to take the risk of altering our way. We make other people's lives unnecessarily tedious by our lack of imagination and consideration. Forgive us through him who was always bringing your forgiving love and healing power to new people in new places.

We also confess, Father, that we are often discontented with the routine which gives us our livelihood. We are too fond of our dreams of doing everything, going everywhere, making the whole world revolve around us. Forgive us through him to whom it was meat and drink to do your will and finish your work.

II

Let us pray:

for men and women in daily life, especially members of our families and those with whom we work, that they may find satisfaction in their work and not be deadened by routine;

for those whose daily work affects the destiny of nations and the welfare of millions, that they may neither take their responsibilities too lightly nor be paralysed by the size and complexity of them;

for those who have to hurt others, and are even employed to kill others in war, that this may never become a matter of routine to them;

for those whose daily work it is to pray and preach and read the Bible, that these activities may not lose their meaning because they are so familiar, but may make ministers more and more sensitive to the claims of the gospel they serve;

for those to whom hard work brings little reward, that the glaring inequalities of life in this world may be removed, at whatever cost to ourselves.

Father, we ask that your will may be done, both in the great creative moments of human life and in its normal daily course.

Sacrifice

I

Lord God, we thank you that we can come to you in our poverty, and yet you accept us. You do not wait to see the size of our gift, nor does your welcome depend upon our merits. You treat us, not as petitioners who must put up a good case, but as children with a secure place in your heart.

It is all too easy for us to take this for granted and presume upon it. Help us to remember what it cost you to treat us in this way. We can only guess at the pain and grief we cause you by the way we repudiate your ideals for us, or give them only lip-service, and by the way we treat one another. We believe the cross of Jesus is the measure both of our shame and of your love. Help us to keep the price of our redemption before us, and make us more ready to serve you, whatever the risk and whatever the cost.

We thank you, Lord, for all the sacrifices men and women make for one another.

We thank you for parents, who put aside their own comfort so that children may be fed and clothed and educated.

We thank you for those who give up their own plans in order to look after sick or elderly relatives.

We thank you for those, killed or injured or made homeless in war, helpless and unwilling victims, who nevertheless suffered that we might live.

We thank you for those who for the gospel's sake have left home, sacrificed prospects, undergone persecution and even laid down their lives.

Above all, we thank you for the death of Jesus, who gave himself that we might cease to crucify each other and our own conscience.

Lord, we acknowledge that we are in debt to very many people.

Help us not to fritter away the life and opportunity which have been so dearly bought for us by so many others. Through Jesus Christ our Lord.

II

Let us recall the words Jesus spoke from the cross.

Father, forgive them: for they know not what they do.
We thank you, Father, that Jesus did as he told others to do, and forgave those who wronged him. Help us to forgive others from our heart. And forgive our world for still committing acts of great cruelty.

Truly, I say to you, today you will be with me in Paradise.
We thank you, Father, that Jesus gave this assurance to a man convinced he deserved to die. Awaken us and all sinners to a true understanding of what we are and what we have done. But give us, too, the same assurance, that whatever we have done nothing can separate us from your love.

Woman, behold your son.   Behold your mother.
We thank you, Father, that Jesus thought of others even when dying. Deliver us from self-pity, from brooding on our own wrongs and misfortunes. Help us to be like Christ to our neighbour, acting as Jesus would act, mediating your love.

My God, my God, why have you forsaken me?
We thank you, Father, that Jesus was fully human, and no stranger to the anguish of despair. Help us also through the dark times, so that we may emerge with faith strengthened.

I am thirsty.
We thank you, Father, that someone answered this cry. Help us to answer the cry of those in our world who are hungry.

It is finished.

We thank you, Father, that Jesus died believing he had done your will and accomplished your work. May we too be single-minded, and when we die not need to regret that we have squandered your gift of life.

Father, into your hands I commit my spirit.

We thank you, Father, that Jesus died trusting fully in you. May all Christians have the same confidence in the hour of death. May all men know that Jesus has conquered death for us all.

Search

I

God, hidden from our eyes,
Men have always been searching for you.
We probe the distances of space;
We plumb the depths of our own minds.
We find you, but never completely.
Left to ourselves we should go on searching for ever.
Only you can bring our search to its goal.

But you have done that:
You have revealed yourself to us in Jesus.
As a baby he was born in a stable at Bethlehem;
As a man he died on a cross at Calvary.
In him our search has reached its goal.

God, hidden from our eyes,
Yet revealed in Jesus Christ,
We worship and adore you.

Father, never before in the history of mankind have we known as
much as we do now. And sometimes, when we see the results of research being used for evil, we wish it had never started. Yet we know
that you want us to search for knowledge, for it is all knowledge about
your world.

Help us always to see our search for knowledge in the right perspec-
tive. Keep reminding us that life is more than facts. And save us from
treating other people merely as objects of study. In our search for
personal life, make us willing to open ourselves to others, and to wait
for them to open themselves to us. And when it comes to knowing you,
we are entirely in your hands. We can know about you only what you
choose to share with us. We thank you for revealing so much of your-

self. Especially we thank you for revealing your innermost being to us in Jesus. Father, keep us receptive, always ready to know you better, through Jesus Christ our Lord.

II

God our Father, you know our dissatisfaction when life falls short of our expectations. Do not let our dissatisfaction lead to despair. May we pursue an active search for fuller and richer life. You are with us in the search – revealing the aim, pointing out the way, and encouraging us to go on.

You are with us in the search for justice and peace. It is a difficult search, for in many cases it seems that we can only have one without the other: peace, at the cost of leaving injustice untouched; or justice, at the cost of a broken peace. Father, show all people how they can strive for justice without recourse to the violence of war; and, if a nation has to go to war, may it not cause more evil than it seeks to remove.

You are with us in the search for economic justice. It is not your will that some should eat well while many go hungry. Bring the rich nations to see that in the long term it is in their interest that all nations should prosper. Save them from reaping short-term advantages at the expense of a future generation's peace. May those in authority not panic when revolution threatens: may they see when a grievance is justified, and act to remove its cause. And may revolutionaries not destroy by their methods the very good they hope to attain.

You are with us in the search for truth. May information not be suppressed. May experts be honest in their presentation of facts and figures and not deliberately mislead the public. And give to all men a desire to get through information to the truth. May we use what we know to create what ought to be.

You are with us in our search for community. A divided society is not your will. May our laws be just to all groups and help to integrate us. May social workers contribute to the making of community life, where all feel wanted and accepted.

Father, our search continues as long as we live. The final goal lies beyond the life we know here. May we be patient and never anxious in our searching, because we know that however many disappointments we have to face, you yourself will not disappoint us.

Senses

I

Eternal God, hidden source and far-glimpsed goal of our lives: when we reflect that all our experience comes to us through the five narrow gateways of our senses, we are filled with new wonder at the way you have made us. By sight and hearing, taste, touch and smell, we find our way through life. By these, also, we find our way towards you, although you are beyond the reach of our senses. The sight of beauty in nature or art; the sound of speech or song or instrument; the touch and smell of polished wood in church; the taste of bread and wine: all these can bring you near in our awareness. Most of all we find you in a look of love or concern on someone's face; in the tone of a trusted voice, the touch of a friendly hand.

Father, from whom we receive all this, save us from turning heaven into hell by treating our sense-experiences as ends in themselves. Keep us thankful and content to have your great gift, even if we must also be often frustrated because the doors of perception are not wider than they are. Show us that if once we have learnt enough of you to find sense a barrier, we are already across the frontier into the realm of eternity, which will endure when our senses have finally failed us.

II

We thank you, Father, that because we can remember and compare, our senses bring to us more than the animals experience. In fear or hopeful expectancy, in satisfaction or disgust, our sensations are gathered up and focused: they become growing-points of character. So we thank you not only for feeling, but for our knowing that we feel: and we pray that our self-knowledge may be both accurate and creative. Make us sensitive and receptive to what goes on around us, so that we experience things not just as outward events but as happening to us.

And let our reaction be one of tolerance and participation, not one of immunity and rejection.

Lord, it is you that have taught us to pray like this. If it were not for the revolution in attitudes which you have brought about through Jesus Christ, we should not have these ideas about involvement and neighbourliness. But we need your further help to turn the ideas into facts of behaviour. May your church never give up saying what it knows about the place of other people in each man's life. May the companies of Christians in each place exhibit a sharing spirit, sensitive to need, and alive to the possibilities of meeting it.

We pray for people who are deprived of sensory perception and expression – the blind, the deaf and the dumb; those who are paralysed; those who have leprosy. If they can be cured, may they not fail of a cure for lack of skilled attention: and if they cannot be cured, may their handicap call forth an abundance of sympathy and help from others.

Eternal God, you are more than the hidden source and far-glimpsed goal of our lives: you are a constant presence, a friend who knows what human existence feels like. May this make a perceptible difference to those who believe it, so that growing numbers of people may come to know you and trust you because of what you are doing today through Jesus Christ our Lord.

Service

Heavenly Father,
There is a silence in the cross.
When the turmoil dies down we are left with nothing but the dreadful
    deed that has been done.
To our lost looking up to heaven there is no answering shout.
You portray power in humility,
    strength in weakness,
    dignity in service;
and we did not know that this could be.
Help us find your kingdom as we serve in quietness.
Through Jesus Christ, our Lord.

Heavenly Father,
We still think of ourselves as more important than others, and squabble
    like children about who is the greatest.
We like to think that people look up to us, and that we really are better
    than they.
But you upset our calculations, and offend against all protocol by
    rolling up your sleeves and coming to serve us.
Help us, please, to forget our old ideas about precedence; let our
    dignity look after itself, and let us find the joy of being useful to
    others.
Through Jesus Christ, our Lord.

Heavenly Father,
It is good to know that our place is to serve, and that this is our
    usefulness.
You do not ask us to worry over motives or results, but quietly, un-
    pretentiously, to do our job in trusting obedience.

Thank you for inviting the church to play its life in this minor key,
    and yet to enjoy the full music of your rule.
Through Jesus Christ, our Lord.

II

Heavenly Father,
    Your coming to us in Christ as servant has turned our ideas round,
and we begin to understand how great it is to serve.

    We pray for our nation, Great Britain, that it may be useful in this
world by actually living out the principles which it has professed. May
it always be hospitable to immigrants, and fair-minded to all minority
groups; consistent in true pleading for justice and peace abroad, and
always ready to help backward or impoverished countries.

    We pray for the mighty nations of America, Russia and China, that
they may succeed in moving from a time of confrontation to concilia-
tion. May they finish with the stockpiling of arms; and may you take
hold of their idealism, and redirect it to the true benefit of mankind.

    We pray for the Middle East: particularly that Israeli and Arab may
come to terms with each other and find happier work in the building
up of shared prosperity.

    We pray for the continent of Africa, that its quickly developing
countries may find their feet in a sane and peaceful world.

    We pray for India, remembering that in modern times it has so
often been cast in the role of peacemaker; that it may continue so, and
at the same time lift its longsuffering poor to a higher and juster
standard of life.

    We pray for Europe, that it may become a true and friendly com-
munity; and for all nations, that we may understand that we belong to
one world, and are created to serve you in freedom.

    Through Jesus Christ, our Lord.

Shelter

I

Eternal Father, men have always looked to you for protection. They have thought of you as a cave to hide in, a harbour to make for, a fort to retreat to. They have thought of you as men think of home, as the place where they ought to be safe, where there is friendship and security.

We thank you that we too can think of you like this, so that we need not pretend, but can admit how weak and frightened life sometimes makes us feel.

Yet we realize we can be over-protected. This can make us lazy: it can keep us weak. So we ask you to help us accept that life is hazardous, learning from Jesus that its chances and dangers have a place in your purpose.

II

Father, we thank you for all that protects us against the elements – for clothing to cover us and buildings to shelter us. We thank you that the worst of our weather rarely threatens us with disaster, and that more and more we can forecast what is coming. Give us practical sympathy, therefore, with those who live in more dangerous parts of the earth, who have to cope with drought and earthquake, flood and hurricane. And make us more grateful to those we depend on who work in all weathers, on our roads, on the farms or out at sea.

We thank you for the imagination and skill of those who design our buildings and plan our towns. Help us to appreciate good architecture. And because we are glad of the safety and comfort of our own homes, make us more willing to devote public money to providing new houses and caring for the homeless.

We thank you for all who provide homes for others: for local auth orities and their housing committees; for building societies, housing associations, and the work of 'Shelter'; those who run hostels and let rooms; those who foster young children. May we all be more neighbourly to lonely people and visitors, remembering the times when others made us welcome.

Heavenly Father, we address these prayers to you through Jesus our Lord, who was exiled in childhood, became homeless to serve you, and invited us to make our home in him.

Simplicity

I

God our Father, we have come to this service by many different roads – in more senses than one. For each of us part of the journey has been along a private road; each of us is ignorant of what the others have been through; and so we cannot help arriving here to a large extent alone.

Yet we meet in one building at one time. May this help us to remember how much we have in common. For whatever the details of our route, we breathe the same air, drink the same water; we touch the same earth, see and hear the same shapes and sounds. We make our way through the same world of feelings – of regret and delight, heartache and buoyancy, jealousy and gratitude.

And in all this we are travelling through your world. It is this which most deeply unites us. So it is fitting that our paths should cross here in your house. For here we can offer you one worship as one people, through our one mediator, Jesus Christ your Son our Lord.

II

Lord our God, we have often heard it said that the first disciples were simple fishermen, and that what Jesus gave them was a simple faith in your love. It makes us think that our faith should be more simple.

But how can we avoid a spurious simplicity, which turns a deaf ear to doubt, and a blind eye to facts which challenge and confuse our faith?

We are not even sure if we want a simple life. Sometimes we yearn for it. But most of the time we want life's refinements as well – the comforts, the luxuries, the complex results of a technology which is anything but simple. And although we sometimes envy our ancestors, we know that it was they who embarked on the journey to complexity, learning new skills, seeking new choices, exploring life in detail.

Even our bodies seem to be against us. For the animal world has developed by endless specialization: and compared with the animals we enjoy what we do because our brains are more intricate than theirs. So how can we reach simplicity without contradicting ourselves?

Lord, in our confusion, help us to learn again from Jesus: to see that his own life was complex, his own choices many; to notice him selecting his priorities, refusing to be distracted, persevering; to hear him, speaking differently to different people, yet always out of the same trust, the same love, the same hope.

Then, though our life is more complicated than his, though we know far more facts and face far more possibilities, help us to see that the key choices have not altered: to address you or to ignore you; to trust you or to despair of you; to serve you or to disengage from you; to share in our Lord's simplicity or to be torn apart by our very abilities.

Spirit

Lord, we worship you as the living Spirit who works in the lives of Christians and in the life of the church, creating anew, bringing new powers to birth, making human actions and characters the bearers of your purpose.

We worship you as the Spirit who makes us aware of our spiritual need and satisfies it.

We worship you as the Spirit who encourages us to live confidently in the world as your children.

We worship you as the Spirit who supports us in our prayers and teaches us how to tell others what Christ means to us.

We worship you as the Spirit who does not allow us to give in to our worse selves but develops truly Christian qualities in us.

We worship you as the Spirit who gives us our varied abilities so that the church may benefit from them.

We worship you as the Spirit who guides the church and draws us into unity with one another.

Help us, Lord the Spirit, to open our lives fully to your influence, and to be the means by which it reaches other people.—

And so we pray,

Lord, we pray that your Spirit may be poured out, not only on those who are already Christians, but on all men.

In a world full of conflicting drives and forces, we pray that your Spirit may take our powers and energies and bring them to fulfilment and harmony in your service, in building and not in destroying.

We pray for all who seek truth, and thus honour you, though as yet unconsciously. May your Spirit make true in their experience what Christ has achieved for all the world.

We pray for people in all those situations of tension and conflict where the welfare of many depends on the integrity of a few. May your Spirit enable men to be honest, and to refuse to put personal advantage above the interests of others.

We pray for the poor and hungry of the world, the ill and the anguished, the dying and the bereaved. May your Spirit distribute both the skill and the love which can bring healing and true comfort.

II

Defend us, Lord, from being Christians in name only. Defend us from conforming outwardly to the standards of Christianity, but not letting its real power enter our lives; from listening to the words of Jesus without obeying him; from being sorry for past failures, yet with no real attempt at improvement.

Help us to work with you and not against you. Save us from being so sure that our ideas are right and our habits good that we cannot even imagine that your will for us might mean changes. And when we do realize what you are calling us to do, help us to trust your wisdom and put ourselves wholeheartedly into your hands.

Help us to please you and not disappoint you. You have honoured us so much in making us your sons and daughters and preparing us to share your eternal life. Do not let us fall away. Do not let us be tempted beyond our strength. Do not let us be lured into a way of life which you cannot bless. Do not let us fritter away our opportunities of doing good. Do not let us rest content with what we have already achieved.

Help us to encourage others and not discourage them. You do not wait until we are perfect before you use us. You do not work only through the learned, the cultured, the mature and the orthodox. Teach us to appreciate simple faith and youthful enthusiasm, even though we may not agree with all that is said and done. May the boldness of others help us to overcome our own timidity.

Help us to control our instinctive desires and to let you direct our lives. May we have done with immorality, and put an end to enmity and rivalry. Produce in us the harvest of the Spirit:

love for you and for one another;
joy in all that you do for us;

peace, because you have forgiven our sins and are in control of everything;

patience in suffering;

kindness, even towards those who are not kind to us;

goodness that is genuine;

faithfulness in all we undertake;

humility, when we compare ourselves with others;

self-control, to make our impulses your servants and not our masters.

Testing

I

God our Father,
life pulls us in many directions,
and presents many possibilities.
Sometimes we do not know which way to turn.
There are so many claims upon our time,
so many demands for our attention,
that the very range of choices before us
drives us to distraction.

It is then that we need you.
Yours is the ultimate claim on our lives;
help us to listen for it in all the other claims that are made on us.
Because we cannot do everything,
help us to get our priorities right,
to know what you want us to do now,
and what we have to leave.

May the stress and strain of life
not break us,
but make us stronger,
for Jesus' sake.

II

Father,
what happens to us is a great test of character,
and our trials leave us the worse or the better,
depending on how we react to them.
We thank you for Jesus:
he was made perfect through sufferings.

Help us, too, to use our trials and sufferings positively,
to face difficult situations
and to make the best of them.

Father, give us sympathetic understanding now as we pray for those
in situations of stress and strain.

We think of those suddenly thrust into a new situation and having to
adapt themselves to a new life
  – young people away from home for the first time,
  – husbands or wives recently widowed,
  – those just retired.
Help them to find their bearings again
  and to discover what changes in themselves you want them to make.

We remember those who feel their lives are spent in a backwater un-
recognized and unacknowledged
  – invalids,
  – children caring for elderly parents,
  – political prisoners.
Save all such from stagnation and boredom.
Keep them lively and alert,
  and bring them to see how their faithfulness has its part in your plan.

We think of people with work-problems
  – those who are stuck with a job they long to change,
  – people living in backward regions with no choice of work,
  – workers made redundant by reorganization,
  – skilled men whose skill is no longer required by society.
Save them all from being embittered,
  and, if they cannot escape, give them the courage they need.

We think of all those who are under great pressure
  – the overworked,
  – those with great responsibilities,
  – mothers with large families,
  – nurses in understaffed hospitals.

Give them the strength they need to see them through
   and save them from being worn out by their work.

Father, we thank you for all your people in the past who have come
   through hard experiences and proved their faith.
Help us, too, to persevere to the end,
   and to use our trials positively and creatively to your glory.

Time

I

Much has happened since we met here last. The days have been full of events great and small. They are the stuff of our lives, the material from which we fashion our worship. We come to you, Father, because you also are involved in these events. You are at home in time as well as in eternity: but because you do not grow old with the flux of time, you give time an eternal significance. This is one of the best things that we know about you.

Yet it has a rough side as well as a smooth. Although we can be sure that we shall not finally be robbed of anything we wish to remember, it means that we must also carry with us what we should prefer to forget. Help us to know and face the whole truth about ourselves, as you know it. Let these passing moments bring to us an awareness of what is really lasting, so that our fears may be calmed and our efforts renewed. We shall not be anxious about tomorrow, since we know that you are neither left behind by growth nor forestalled by decay, but are in all things without being subject to them. This you have confirmed to us in Jesus Christ. He is with us always, to the end of time: in him our labour cannot be lost, for you and he are one. Glory to you for ever.

II

To be conscious of time is humanity's hallmark. All our awareness depends on this. Remembering, looking forward, comparing moment with moment, we experience hope and fear, satisfaction and regret, pain and delight. For all these, and our capacity to learn and forgive, we praise you, Father. For language and music which depend on succession of sounds in time; for the sense of continuity and personal identity, which enables us to practise detachment or make new starts without fear of getting separated from ourselves; for the excitement of first discoveries and the delight of recognizing what is familiar, we thank you.

And above all these great blessings we thank you for the rare moments of intense awareness when time seems to stand still for us, and we can hardly tell if a minute has passed or an hour. In such moments you give us hints and foretastes of the rapture of eternity.

Yet even these, like the rest of our times, are ambiguous. It can as readily be fright that stops the clock for us as pleasure. But eternity is not like that: for eternity is yourself, and the message we have heard from Jesus is that you are all light and no darkness. There is nothing ambiguous or variable about your love and forgiveness.

We rejoice in your constancy, and pray that the experience of it may illuminate those whose path lies at present through moving and menacing shadows. Married couples upon whose first love the years have weighed too heavily. Workers to whom routine has become, instead of a liberation, a nightmare of imprisonment or numbness. Those burdened with the knowledge of wasted time, missed opportunities. Those for whom days and months drag interminably, offering no end to boredom, or frustration, or apprehension. Those also for whom there is not time enough, and who approach the end of each day, or of all their days, with tasks unfinished and plans unfulfilled.

Father, we fall easily into the habit of thinking that time goes in circles. The seasons pass and return; all earthly things are renewed in the cycle of birth and death; civilizations rise and fall, giving place to others. But in your dealings with men, and above all in Jesus, we have come to know that you have a purpose; that things do not just recur but are moving onwards towards your goal. May we, in our daily round, take our place in the unfolding history of love whose line does not stop short at death, cut off there, but leads through into the timeless blessedness of completion. And may we even there, in ways beyond all imagining, possess and exercise the faculty to remember and to recognize, since it is part of your own eternal nature revealed to us in Jesus Christ our Lord.

Tragedy

I

Lord Jesus Christ, we pause to see you dying on the cross, and to take in what it means . . . No one person was responsible for your death: priests, governor, soldiers, betrayer, mob – all bear some responsibility, but in the tangled situation not one of them was wholly to blame. That is the tragedy – all the actors in it seem to be caught up helplessly in the course of events. You freely decided to go to Jerusalem knowing what was waiting for you there, but now that you are there, events seem to have taken over, and even you seem helpless. It is tragic when people lose control of the situation, and goodness and love get crucified. Help us to take in this whole tragedy and to marvel at your love and patience through all the suffering and pain.

God our Father, the cross of Christ stands in our path, making us stop and realize that we have contributed to the tragedy of the world. There are many evils for which we cannot personally be blamed, and yet we are caught up in the situations which create them. We know that we share in the blame for the hunger of the world because of the economic system in which we play a part. We know that wars continue because governments representing us wage them or do not take effective measures to prevent them. We feel our guilt and yet we do not know how to extricate ourselves from it. Like all those caught up in the crucifixion story, we are enmeshed in the system. We are on the side of the crucifiers. Today, Father, as we consider the suffering of Christ make us sure enough of your forgiveness to play our true part in curing what we have helped to cause. Jesus was involved in human life without becoming a victim to all the pressures placed upon him; help us to do the same, even when we have to suffer for it. We want to be on the side of the Crucified.

God our Father, when tragedy confronts us, especially when we can find no cause for it, we find it difficult to believe that you are in control of things. It seems as if you stand aside to let it happen; but the cross of Jesus reminds us that when it comes you are there right in the middle of it. Help us never to forget that, when we consider all the sadness in the world.

There is the tragedy of children born handicapped; it is a tragedy from which we turn in horror, and yet, Lord, if we dare to look, you are there. You bring people to accept the reality of the situation, and your presence can be seen in the patience of the handicapped and in the love of those who care.

There is the tragedy of those who know that their lives will be short; the rest of us doubt whether we would have the courage to live with that knowledge, and yet in this tragedy, too, you are present. Your example gives the dying courage in the face of death and helps us all to see that the quality of life is not to be judged by its length on earth.

There is the tragedy of those who have lived too long, who have outlived family and friends, are worn out and yet do not die. Help them to be patient and to find you in the love and concern of those around them.

There is the tragedy of those suddenly bereaved. We easily feel that if you had been there, it would not have happened. But even in such a tragedy, you are there. You bring comfort to the grief-stricken and help them to pick up the threads of life again.

There is the tragedy of those who have caused tragedy in the lives of others, and who are now burdened by the thought of the damage they have done. We remember those involved in car accidents who have survived while others have not. We know how people in such circumstances find it difficult to forgive themselves. Father, bring your forgiveness home to them and ease their burdened consciences.

There is the tragedy of those whose personalities are warped, whose upbringing and experiences have harmed them, and who can so easily be brought to ruin by flaws of character. May your love heal the wounds in their personalities so that, even though scars remain, they may not further harm themselves. May people surround them with love and understanding, and so make you real to them.

Father, we are reminded daily of the pain there is in the world. It would be so easy and natural for us to refuse to face reality or to protect ourselves by becoming callous or hard. Help us to keep our hearts tender, sensitive to the pain and sorrow of others, always careful not to cause a tragedy or make it worse by our actions. Just as someone quenched the thirst of our Lord by giving him a drink, help us to do what we can to comfort the afflicted and so serve Christ.

Triumph

I

Today, Lord, we give you thanks for the victories of our Lord Jesus Christ.

We thank you that these were real victories, won in the dust and heat of our human struggle.

We thank you that they were victories of love, won not by the sword but by patience in well-doing and by endurance of evil.

We thank you that they were victories not for himself alone, but for the benefit of the whole human race.

We thank you for his victory over suffering and pain, his power to release people from the bondage of crippling disease, and to make them more than conquerors over hardships.

We thank you for his victory over sin, disarming it and setting the sinner on a new course.

We thank you for his victory over death, enabling people to fall asleep in the sure knowledge of the resurrection to eternal life.

Because he is still the world's great champion and conqueror, we gladly own our debt to him and our allegiance to him.

II

We who have given thanks for Christ's victories now pray for his victory in the life of the world today.

We pray that the gospel of our Lord Jesus Christ may be known and believed by increasing numbers of men and women. May young and old, rich and poor, of every race, nation and language, realize what Christ has done for them and join their praise with that of the whole church.

We pray that we who follow Christ may manifest his victory in our way of life. May we be strong where we have been weak, compassionate where we have been hard, generous where we have been selfish, whole-hearted where we have been lukewarm.

We pray that the influence of Christ may reach beyond professed Christians to affect the whole life of society. May the ideals of peace and justice and care for each other be written on all our hearts, and may we not rest until these become the normal standards of the world.

We pray that Christ may strengthen men and women in their trials: in sickness, in bereavement, in hardship, in persecution, in disappointment.

May the victorious Christ strengthen us all to endure and conquer in his name.

Water

I

Let us thank God for water.

God our Father, you have created us and created the world in your wisdom. We marvel at how many uses simple things can have. We thank you now especially for water. It so quickly and completely quenches our thirst. It falls into the ground and enables innumerable crops and plants to live and to support life. We can wash in it and swim in it. It keeps our streets clean, puts out fires, generates electricity. And then the sight and sound of streams and rivers, waterfalls and lakes, the sea and the rain can take our breath away and invigorate us again. We thank you, Lord, for this great gift.

But water can be destructive and terrifying. Torrential rain, floods, storms at sea – these present water as sinister, a threat to our existence. Sometimes it has been seen as the instrument of your judgment; sometimes it has seemed rather to represent blind chaos. We who have seen your majesty in Christ cannot identify you with the fury of the elements. We who have heard Jesus say, 'Peace, be still', cannot believe that they are out of your control. Help us, when we are up against the forces of nature, and when we go through deep waters of the spirit, to believe that you are on our side, and that they cannot sweep us away.

II

Let us remember some of the things water stands for in the Bible.

We must all die, we are like water spilt on the ground, which cannot be gathered up again. Help us, Lord, to remember the preciousness and frailty of human life, and to try to give every person his chance to live fully. We pray that the people of .... may be spared the waste and suffering of war. We pray that those who are imprisoned for conscience's sake may not be made to waste their best years.

Waters shall break forth in the wilderness, and streams in the desert. We pray for the many people in the world who find it hard to make a living from the soil, however hard they work; and we ask that the skill of engineers and the knowledge of advisers may be put readily at their disposal, backed by the resources of the West, ungrudgingly given.

Whoever gives to one of these little ones even a cup of cold water, he shall not lose his reward. We remember all those who have shown us kindness, in great ways and small; and we ask for the sympathy which is quick to meet the needs of others.

I will sprinkle clean water upon you, and you shall be clean. We could not live without the assurance that Christ has cleansed us from our sins, and we ask for grace to persevere in the new life he has given us.

He leads me beside still waters. The peace of God keeps our hearts, and we ask that the people we know, our families, our friends, our neighbours, the people with whom we work, especially any who are ill or in trouble, may also find that peace and so gain strength to live to God's glory.

(*II Samuel 14.14; Isaiah 35.6; Matthew 10.42; Ezekiel 36.25; Psalm 23.2: RSV*)

Way

I

Father, we cannot help thinking of our life as a journey. It is not just a cycle of birth, growth, maturity and decay. We are travelling from our origins towards our destiny. We hope to arrive somewhere better than we set out from.

You are our destination. Not that we start far from you: for you are there in our heredity, in our earliest environment. But we can only reach you by setting out to come to you. It is only as we attempt the course that we realize how rewarding it is.

We know the way. It is through Jesus that we come to you. It is by following him, obeying him, identifying ourselves with him, suffering with him, rising with him that we receive direction and find the route. Help us not to hesitate, and not to wander away from the path, but to keep to the course he has travelled.

II

We thank you, Father, that we are helped on the way to you by the experience of other travellers.

We thank you for what we know of the first disciples, their early failures and subsequent achievements in Christ's name.

We thank you for the martyrs and saints whose story encourages us both to act and to endure for the gospel's sake.

We thank you for those whose writings, in the Bible and in other books, recall us to perseverance.

We thank you for all those known to us who have pressed steadily onwards despite the worries and distractions and tedium of everyday life.

We pray for young people as they set out on the journey. We are often anxious lest they should miss the right road. Help them to find the narrow gate that leads to life, to count the cost and not to look back.

We pray for people as they settle into their careers and set up home. May they not be lured from the path by dazzling prospects. May they be willing to trudge when early enthusiasm begins to die down.

We pray for the middle-aged, as the way becomes all too familiar, and the prospects are outweighed by the realities. May they renew their strength as they turn to you, run without wearying, walk without feeling faint.

We pray for the elderly, as they reach the last stretches of the road. May they receive the support they need, and may their experience serve to encourage younger people along the road. Give them a clear vision of the destination and may they be unafraid because you are their guide.

Lord, do not let anyone be missing at journey's end. Bring us all safely home to your presence.

Witness

I

God our Father,
    You have never left yourself without witness.
    The world of nature testifies to your power;
    In the world of men your love and your justice are to be seen.

Lord Jesus Christ,
    Witness to the Father's love,
    Yours is the vital and crucial evidence.
    You are the key witness pointing men and women
    to the truth about God and man.

Holy Spirit of Jesus,
    Witness within the hearts and minds of men,
    You also encourage us to give evidence on Jesus' behalf.

God, Father, Son and Spirit, help us to be effective witnesses to you,
    through Jesus Christ our Lord.

Father, we know that you have appointed us to demonstrate the reality of your love in our lives and words. Yet we confess that we have often given more evidence of our own selfishness than of your power to transform our personalities. Forgive us. Help us to point away from ourselves to the reality of your love. May our actions and words convince people of the truth as it is in Jesus.

II

Father, we thank you for all your faithful witnesses of past days who have testified to your living presence.
    We praise you for the prophets who pointed forward to your coming
      in Jesus;

for the apostles who carried their witness to him throughout the world,

and for the Bible which today points us to Christ.

We remember with gratitude those who first brought the gospel to our land, and those who by their witness have brought us to faith.

We thank you for the martyrs whose witness has been made by their death, and for all your people who have faithfully borne witness to you in their lives.

Father, help us in our turn to be good witnesses.

Father, as we thank you for your witnesses in the past, we cannot forget those who are your witnesses today. We thank you for those who have gone to lands other than their own. Help them to understand the people they live among, to be true to you and by the way they live and the words they speak to point men and women to Jesus Christ.

We think of all Bible translators, especially those putting languages into a written form for the first time. Help them in their task, so that through the written testimony provided by scripture men and women may come to faith in Jesus Christ.

We think of all ministers of the gospel. By the way they live, the words they speak, and the care they have for people, may they be a living demonstration of your love and power.

We think of those who suffer opposition or persecution because of their witness to you. Keep them faithful, so that their patience in suffering may point people to the suffering and patience of Christ.

Father, we are your people, and you appoint us all to be your witnesses before the world; it is we who provide the evidence on which the world judges. May we provide the evidence that is needed, so that others may come to believe in you through Jesus Christ our Lord.

Wonder

I

Heavenly Father,
We praise you for the wonder of your eternal being:
from you originates this vast creation, to run its course, and pass away.

We praise you for the wonder of our birth –
    in your mind were we lovingly conceived for a reason precious to
        yourself,
    and consecrated to your purpose in Christ.
We praise you for the wonder of our life –
    through your patience we are given the means of salvation
    to work out with joy.
We praise you for the wonder of our dying –
    that in this final way we are able to give you back the charge of our
        life,
    which only you can complete.

And yet we confess that we are so prosaic –
    accepting life casually and drifting from one circumstance to
        another
    simply to fade out when our time comes.
Please give us a sense of wonder and bring us to the experience of awe
    which the early Christians had.

II

Almighty God,
You are too much for us.
    You break out of our dogmas and churches, and move through this
        creation in exultant joy.
    You disturb us; you waken us, and now, we are restlessly aware
        of you.

And yet your love reassures us.
  You have opened our eyes wide in wonder, but we learn that we are
    your children, and may tiptoe through this wondrous life in trust.

Almighty God,
Man looks at himself; his origins, his world, his future:
  and he looks to you, and wonders.

He sees his beginning in the humbling chain of evolution, as one
  amongst many of your creative marvels, and longs to believe in your
  plan.
He feels his position on the edge of this vast universe, and looks to
  other worlds in outer space, and hesitates, with a pause of belief and
  unbelief.
He looks to the future, and loses himself in the incomprehensible
  stretch of time.
He turns in great relief to Christ, and holds to him, pivot in the
  wheeling movement of creation. Now he is filled with trembling
  joy, as he dares to believe that out of the present anguish of this
  whole order shall come steady bliss.

We pray for man in his day
  through Jesus Christ, our Lord.

Words

I

Heavenly Father,

We marvel that you should concern yourself with us, and that you should wish to communicate with us. But the greatest marvel of all is that you have spoken to us in Christ.

He is the authentic word which conveys the truth,

the single word which consolidates wisdom,

the direct word which comes to the point.

In him you speak in a way which gets through to us. Please make us listen, for our sanity's sake.

Heavenly Father,

We thank you that in Jesus you talk to us as no one else can. You plumb the depths of our despair and yearning, and speak in answer to our lonely need. Through him, you converse with us, and mediate yourself.

We thank you too that he has become the mediator between us and others – the very channel of communication and ground of friendship. Now we can talk with all in the true tones of understanding, through Jesus Christ, our Lord.

II

Heavenly Father,

In Christ, you have broken for ever the silence of creation, and begun with man a conversation which must lead into deep friendship: but we break off communication with our fellows when we please, and must confess that we have, seemingly, preferred the silence which breeds misunderstanding and hate.

In Christ, you have ended all ambiguity, but we are so glib; we try, by our eloquence, to bring together what is false and what is true, and make our words tell half-truths and lies.

In Christ, you speak with an economy which reduces wisdom to simplicity; but we use our words without care, so that they are blunted in their meaning, and we lose a real regard for truth.

In Christ, you speak a word which reconciles, and builds up; but we use words to hurt and to destroy.

Father, we thank you for your precious word to us in Jesus, spoken with care, and at great cost.

Teach us how to talk to one another in truth, and not to put our words to waste.

Heavenly Father,

We thank you for giving us words to speak, and pray for ourselves and all who misuse this gift.

We pray for those who take no delight in conversation, who stone-wall the advances of others, and slow down all communication.

We pray for those who let their tongues run away with them in idle gossip, who talk themselves silly, and for all their many words say nothing.

We pray for those who talk to impress, and even to keep others at a distance, by bombarding them with long monologues of prejudice and self-justification, and never stop to listen.

We pray for those who use words, not to enlighten, but to conceal the truth, and put off the day of action – lying words, by which they not only fool others but deceive themselves.

We praise you that already, by your Spirit, you speak on man's behalf with sighs too deep for words, and pray that all may find speech to echo your thoughts.

Through Jesus Christ, our Lord.

Work

I

Eternal Father, we worship you between one week's work and another's; and we cannot remember our work without feeling both glad and ashamed: glad about the good work we did last week, and ashamed that so much of it was less than our best.

It is not just that sometimes we were lazy, disagreeable, jealous, even dishonest; but that half the time our motives were so muddled. We were trying to earn money, trying to win praise, trying to satisfy customers, or at least avoid getting told off. And in all these ways it was simply a means to an end. Only rarely did we think of our work as something to be done for its own sake, or as a way of using some ability we were glad to possess.

And this not only made our work harder than it need have been; it was a poor preparation for coming to church today. It put us in danger of thinking of worship as another kind of work, a duty we owe you, an effort we make to win your approval.

Help us to realize that we have your approval before we begin; that you pay us your love in advance, not in arrears; and that the point of our worship is neither to give you anything you need, nor to offer you praise in exchange for your love, but to use an ability we are glad to possess, to thank, to trust, to ask and to receive.

Lord, may our worshipping frame of mind transform our work. Then we can gratefully use the abilities you have given us, and willingly share with others in enriching your world; and this too will be our worship.

II

Eternal God, you created the world full of potential. We thank you that in making us in your image, you made us capable of realizing some of this potential by our work. Despite what we often say, we are glad there is work for us to do.

So we cannot help praying for those who are unable to work: for the ill and the permanently injured; those who by their own and society's fault have become inefficient, or work-shy, or unemployable; the men who in later years find their hard-won skills no longer wanted, who fear takeovers or the rationalization of their industry, who feel threatened with redundancy or long-term unemployment.

We pray too, therefore, for those who bear the responsibility for choosing and directing the changes in our working lives: those engaged in work study, in management training, in the reform of bargaining procedures and the redeployment of manpower. Save them equally from the idealism which ignores our competitiveness, and from the cynicism which assumes we shall never be generous. May their aim be not only to make us efficient but, however impersonal a man's actual work may be, to make the place where he works a more personal place.

We pray for ourselves as Christians, that what we believe may find expression in our working day: that we may be easy to work with, a good influence on those who begin their working lives with us, and dependable in small things as well as large. If we have power, may we be straightforward in our use of it; if we are married, may we be fair to both our work and our home; when we have to compromise, may it be in the general interest and not just our own; and when we receive promotion, may we remember that we still have a Master in heaven.

Index of Intercessions

Accident, victims of, 42, 99
Administrators, educational, 26, 66
  welfare, 56
Agriculturalists, 6
Aid, overseas, 6, 56, 85, 104
Anguish, 44, 77, 91, 110
Anxiety, 18, 73, 81, 114

Beggars, 10, 114
Bereaved, 18, 91, 94, 99, 102
Boredom, 71, 97
Broadcasters, 8, 54

Challenge, 18
Children, 30, 44, 48, 68, 76, 87, 94
Church, compassionate, 28, 40, 100,
  101-102
  confident but not arrogant, 46
  creating community, 10, 61, 102
  dual citizenship, 2
  embodying Christ, 44, 77, 83, 108
  in education, 25-26
  instrument of protest and reform,
    8, 102
  in various lands and cultures, 14,
    76, 108
  leaders, 6, 22
  living by faith, 28
  ministers, 75, 108
  opening up possibilities, 61
  persecuted, 76, 108
  preachers, 54, 75
  proclaiming love, 32, 83
  recognizing new needs, 56, 83, 104
  respecting privacy, 10
  theologians, 6
  translators, 108
  travelling light, 4
  unions, 68
  unity, 68
Civil servants, 6, 36, 59
Colleges, 26
Commerce, leaders of, 8, 36, 56
Community, 10, 61, 80, 102
Councillors, 9-10

Decision-makers, 53, 90-91
Despised, 60
Developing countries, 6, 56, 85
Disappointment, 42, 73, 102
Dislike, those whom we, 2
Distaste, 2
Dying, 78, 91, 99, 109

Economic systems and forces, 28, 59,
  65, 80, 98
Educationally subnormal, 26
Elderly, 12, 63, 68, 76, 94, 99, 101,
  106
Employers, 54
Engineers, 6, 104
Entertainers, 71
Equality, 55-56, 68, 75
Evil, dupes of, 2, 40, 73
Exploited, 50, 65, 71, 75

Family, 4, 22, 26, 29-30, 42, 75, 94, 104
Farmers, 86
Fear, 8, 17-18, 20, 22, 50, 73, 78, 86, 97, 103, 106, 114
Fishermen and seamen, 86
Friends, 104
Frustration, 97

Gossip, 112
Government, the, 22, 35, 56, 59, 65, 80

Handicapped, 10, 26, 83, 99, 114
Homeless and poorly housed, 10, 28, 39, 44, 60, 86-87
Hospitals, etc., 38, 94
Hungry, 5-6, 29, 39, 44, 51, 60, 63, 77, 80, 91, 98

Ill, and those who care for and heal, 10, 11, 18, 29, 38, 42, 63, 76, 91, 102, 104, 114
Illiterate, 26
Immigration and customs control, 5, 34, 85
Industry, leaders of, 8, 36, 54, 66, 114
Influence, those tempted to misuse, 34, 91, 112
Information, availability of, 65, 80
International relations, 4, 20, 28, 59, 61, 68, 85
  trade and currency, 5-6, 56, 65
Invalids, 94

Journalists, 8
Judges, 34
Justice, 4, 6, 28, 40, 80, 85, 102

Legislators, 8, 80
Lepers, 83
Limited in outlook, 48, 73
Local authorities, 86-87
Lonely, 38, 87, 111

Magistrates, 34
Mankind, 15, 48, 67, 73, 90, 110
Married, 22, 29-30, 68, 97, 106, 114
Middle-aged, 106
Minorities, 12, 34, 51, 65, 80, 85
Murderers, 18, 51

Nation, our, 28, 85
Nations, leaders of, 53, 59, 65, 85, 90
Neighbourhood, 4, 83, 104

Obsolescence, planned, 65
Opposition to government, etc., 34, 65

Parents, 22, 68, 76, 94
Peace, 4, 14, 20, 28, 39, 68, 80, 85, 102
Persecuted, 51, 102, 108
Planners, 34, 97
Police, 34, 75
Politicians, 6, 20, 22, 36, 59
Prejudiced, 112
Prisoners, past or present, 10, 12, 28, 29, 34
  political, 12, 34, 65, 66, 94, 103
Public servants, 10, 36, 38
Publicists, 65, 80

Racial discrimination and reconciliation, 10, 51, 64, 68
Religions, reconciliation between, 45, 61, 68
Resources, right use of, 15, 58

Retired, 94
Revolution, 80, 83, 85

Schools, 26
Scientists, 53
Slaves, 34, 65
Social workers, 80
Speakers, 54, 66
Students, 26
    leaders of, 26
Sunday, use of, 71

Tax officers, 56
Teachers, 8, 26, 54
Test, those brought to the, 18, 53
Thieves, 18
Trade, boards of, 6
    terms of, 5-6, 56, 65
    unions, 66, 114
Tragedy, those who cause, 99
Transport workers, 86
Tribunals, 34
Trouble, those in, 104
Truth, those who seek, 79, 80, 90
Tyranny, those who live under, 36,
    65

Unbelievers, 16, 62-63, 101, 108
Uncertain, 18, 28, 110
Uncommunicative, 112
Unemployed, 10, 65, 71, 114
Universe, 15, 109-110
Universities, 26
Unruly, 36

Visitors, 87
Voluntary service, 56

War, armaments for, 50, 53, 85
    killers in, 75, 80
    victims of, 63, 65, 76, 103
Warped personalities, 99
Work, 3-4, 22, 24, 71, 75, 94, 97, 104,
    114
World, one, 14, 20, 39, 50-51, 68, 85,
    88, 90
Writers, 8, 66
Wrong, those who seek ways of
    righting, 22, 46, 64-66

Young, 12, 22, 48, 68, 94, 101, 105-
    106